America's Fastest Way To Become A Millionaire!

"The Magic Nine System!"

by
Mark J. Reynolds

Library of Congress Cataloging in Publication Data
Mark J. Reynolds

TITLE: America's Fastest Way To Become A Millionaire
          I. Title.

ISBN 0-915451-06-9

Manufactured in the United States of America
9 8 7 6 5 4 3 2 1

TABLE OF CONTENTS
"The Magic Nine System"

Come Along For "The Magic Nine System" **Millionaires** Bus Ride. When you get off, You Just May Be Rich.

There is Always Room For One More Millionaire At The Top; You May Be Next

Warning! The book that you are now holding, in your hands, can and will absolutely change your life. From this day forward you will never wonder what it's like to be a millionaire; you will be one.

These two Millionaire-Making Programs described in "AMERICA'S FASTEST WAY TO BECOME A MILLIONAIRE" means exactly what it says.

If you have been looking for a Magic Formula, a simple recipe, with no ifs or buts to it, that will make you a millionaire. Then that's what these two programs will do for you. But don't be surprised when it works for you, right now, out of your own home, because it's designed to do just that.

If there is one thing I have learned, over the past ten years, from personal experience as well as observation, it is that there is a MAGIC FORMULA. A Magic Formula so great that most people, who know about it, will not even tell their families much less the general public. If you ask them, there is a standard line they will recite you without even blinking an eye. "Becoming successful in business is the result of many different things or a combination of all of them, luck, timing, knowing the right people, single-mindedness, an understanding of human nature, the ability to think big, and the courage to take calculated risks." To that I say, BUNK. I say if you choose one of the programs I have described, in detail, in this book and put in an honest effort, you will be a millionaire before the year is out.

1

Believe it or not, it's your choice, but I'll tell you this, more people in America have become millionaires in the last five years by using one of these formulas than any other way known to man. And the funniest part about the formula is that most of the people who became millionaires were from poor families.

Horatio Alger, the author of one of the most widely read self-help books of all time, maintained that the key to becoming RICH was hard work and more hard work. But there are millions of people around the world and in America who have worked like demons all their lives without getting anywhere at all. Then there are a great many people who follow a simple formula, like the ones I have provided, that have made absolute fortunes with the minimum of effort. Alger himself died flat broke.

Then comes the worst of them all, parents and school teachers who seem like they spend most of their adult lives persuading the young to accept the CLASSIC MYTH: "That academic accomplishments will automatically lead to financial success." It doesn't work that way at all. Most academically brilliant young men and women make very little money throughout their lifetime no matter how hard they work. High school dropouts often make a great deal more.

Larry Wright, the founder of the shoe company that bears his name, told me a few years ago in Boston, that he was a very poor student in school, and at the age of fifteen he had to leave school to help out the family. Today he is a millionaire many times over operating a very successful mail order import shoe company. He told me, the last time I ran into him, that if he had to take the current examination for his own company he would probably fail. Ironic, isn't it?

Recent history is full of people who, in their youth, seemed unlikely candidates for Millionaire status, and today are worth a small fortune.

The following stories are about three friends who I shared this information with before I wrote "America's Fastest Way To Become A Millionaire," people, maybe not unlike yourself, who started with limited funds utilizing one of the formulas in this book and who now have a thriving profitable business.

I don't believe in looking back, but my wife sometimes remembers when our only "good times" used to seem gone with our youth. These days our happiness is in the present and the future looks even brighter. But she's right, it wasn't always so cozy.

We both used to have perfectly good "outside" jobs and, when we first got married, we thought we were doing pretty well. We weren't doing so badly, but it seemed we were on the losing end of time. Time was moving forward, but we weren't. We were crawling along while the rest of the world was booming. We simply made up our minds to be a part of the boom.

There might have been countless routes to the wealth and independence we have now. Calling our own shots with our own business appealed to us. But we didn't have rich relatives or a winning lottery number at hand. We wanted to move swiftly, but without the insecurity of leaving the "good" jobs we had. The answer, obviously and unquestionably, was our own home mail order business. We even set up our first goal: $250,000 in six months. By the time we had that, we figured both of us could quit working.

Now, I was no handy-man and my wife didn't knit. So, lacking a trade, we couldn't produce what we would sell. The wholesale prices of products sold by local wholesalers didn't allow enough profit margin to really pay off. The duplication and competition in the many mail-order catalogs would have stopped us before we started.

Thank God for our friend *Mark J. Reynolds.* He showed the right direction to take. Here's how we got started:

For the price of a few phone calls and postage stamps we obtained the names and addresses of overseas manufacturing corporations the same ones that are listed in the back of this book. These manufacturers overflowed with products in demand and unusual items that had little exposure on the U.S. market. The profits available from the inexpensive sources made it possible for us to start small. We tested our products and remained flexible.

We started with our instincts. My wife knew that ladies'

3

shoes and handbags always had captive audiences in department and specialty stores. I have an eye for ladies' fashions and I knew everyone likes to look at well dressed women. Soon, we weren't short on ideas, just action. *Mark* showed us how to write our own ads and we learned how to advertise when the rates were cheap, when magazines were offering space advertising rates at low, low prices. We picked one product and a back-up: a pair of ladies' shoes and an imported imitation leather handbag.

Our first small advertising campaign was a modest cost. Our two stage marketing plan was a FREE OFFER in the space ad for more information on our products and a direct mail package mailed to the potential customers who responded to our ad. The response soon proved profitable. We had more orders than we could fill, so we quickly re-ordered more inventory. Our third stage of planning, Add-More-Products To Our Line, went into action even sooner than we thought. We added five more products to be included in our new "Small but powerful" catalog. More time was soon needed to keep pace with importing and selling. My wife and I literally flipped a coin to see who would stay home! She WON! And all that happened in just six months - we'd reached the first half of our goal.

Well today, we both operate our own business in small offices and one warehouse, just outside of Chicago, and we are happy to tell the world; we punch no man's time clock.

The few hundred dollars we spent to set up our business in the garage and the kitchen, in the beginning, was well worth it. The modest investment in merchandise from Hong Kong and Taiwan became thousands of dollars in sales in the first few months. The product line grew, the quantity of our mailing list soared, and after the first year we became wholesale suppliers for retailers in addition to our small mail order company. This isn't one of those get rich quick stories. We applied a few careful techniques given to us by *Mark* and our own determination. You can't do without either one of those ingredients, but if you have to learn on the way, it's the determination to succeed that you must have. There were many routes we could have gone, like I said. Our "secret" is *Mark J. Reynolds* and our determination to own our own business.

4

Sincerely,

Mr. & Mrs. A. O'Brien
Chicago, Ill.

Success Story Number Two

How did I get into my own successful "back room" mail order business? I was a very capable salesperson in a local retail store. Everything changed when the boss said he was going out of business and I was fired. The store had failed to keep pace with the times. The new mall down the street was where all the action was.

I didn't know it at the time, but getting fired was the best thing that could have happened to me. Oh, I was able to pick up other store work easily enough, at the new mall, but I was determined to not let getting fired disrupt my life again. Sure, I had a paycheck again, but I felt I'd only switched cars on the same train. I wanted my own train! I knew all along I had some of the practice and knowledge needed to make it on my own, but I needed getting fired to get me started!

My old boss used to talk about getting into the mail-order business. We talked about it sometimes, he never did it. I decided I'd try my wings at it myself. I had the store job for a little income, so I figured I could start out working from my home. But what to sell? One thing seemed as good as another; little did I know there was a big difference.

Then, at work, I couldn't help but notice a store that sold dolls and stuffed animals, just dolls and stuffed animals. Their business was booming. The item and "its time," I guess. Maybe I didn't know anything about dolls or teddy bears or how to import them from the far east, but I knew a lot about people and sales. Conversations with people working in that store taught me "basic doll:" different types, their names, materials, styles, sizes, prices, and so on.

5

But what I learned from *Mark Reynolds,* my former college friend, was there was a big difference in importing the dolls direct from Hong Kong than buying them from California wholesalers. Here is a little insight into how I began:

I found that there are incredibly inexpensive dolls and stuffed animals in the Far East markets. In Hong Kong, I found the most popular doll models sold wholesale for $1.43 and fetched a premium stateside price of $19.95. Savings from just a couple of months pay enabled me to buy my first shipment of dolls. I placed a small, inexpensive 3'' by 3'' ad with three magazines: *Craft Magazine, 1001 Home Ideas, and McCall's Ladies Magazine.*

By the time I had sold half of my first batch of dolls, I already had enough profit to buy another shipment. I also had enough money to run the ad again in the same three magazines. Within the first six months I had purchased more dolls two more times and increased my advertising budget. I also added two more publications from *Marks* recommmended list of magazines: Better Homes & Garden and New Shelter. I added two additional doll styles to my product line plus some small stuffed dogs. And, thanks to the profit margin in Far East purchasing-stateside selling, I still had profits left over.

I began direct mail solicitation to my customer mailing list and offered more stuffed animals and related Christmas items that I could see sold well in the stores. Since I had an average salary still coming in, I used all the doll profits to expand my product line and the advertising program.

I suddenly realized I had the whole train! I'd made more money in three months than I had made in the last two years working for someone else. My pay from work at the store and the profits from my own mail-order company allowed me continual expansion of my new business. I didn't need to keep depending on an employer to stay in business just so I could keep my job. The growth of the business excited me and I found the marketing fun. Along with dolls and stuffed animals, I've added other small toys to my product line.

My business had quickly outgrown the spare bedroom at home. I moved the whole operation into a small warehouse in a nearby industrial park. Of course, I had to quit work at the mall, but there's no end to what I can now do for myself. Thanks Mark Reynolds.

Sincerely,

D. G. Silverman
Fountain Valley, CA

Success Story Number Three

I never thought I'd be my own businessman, run my own shop, so to speak, but I wanted to do something on the side. I felt like a hobbyist without a hobby. So, extra money wasn't the reason I got into my mail order business that I operate from home. And actually, I hardly run it from my home anymore. It got big enough to afford a small office for itself and have its own workers.

I was never a TV buff or did much with the spare time between shifts at the personnel office where I worked. In the summer, when the weather was good, I liked hiking and fishing, but I couldn't do that year 'round. During the off-season I was at loose ends. I couldn't pass all my time tying a few new flies, designing a lure, outfitting and re-outfitting my tackle box and gear.

A friend of mine, *Mark J. Reynolds,* once complimented me on the success of one of my fishing lures. I gave it to him and made another for myself. Later, he said it worked so well I should sell it, via Mail-Order, and make a fortune. Well, I didn't know about that. I was knee deep in kids and never seemed to find an end to the work around our small farm. But another time, when we were at the small local tackle and bait shop, *Mark* pushed me up to the counter and tried to sell the store owner on the lure. He wasn't interested, said he had plenty of flies and lures from big supply houses.
It was embarrassing.

And it got my dander up. I actually brooded for a couple of days. But, with my usual spare time, I began to think about things. I made several lures, wrote a simple, clear ad, and phoned my favorite fishing magazine to ask about their

7

advertising rates. Well, it was in-season and the rates were high. I began to realize I'd have to make and sell a ton of lures just to pay for the advertising. And what about materials and my time?

I was discouraged, but I decided to get wise. I contacted *Mark* and he put me in touch with an advertising agency in California. They showed me how to get big discounts on advertising rates. Then *Mark* showed me how to import fishing products from Taiwan. He typed out a complete guide to manufacturing companies in the Taiwan that listed hundreds of manufacturers that sold fishing poles, reels, and other supplies for outdoorsmen.

I decided to import and sell from home. I enjoyed the phone calls, the figuring. I knew fishermen. And I had time. For every forty hours at the office, I had easily another twenty hours at home. The bug had bit me. Time that I used to kill, working around the farm, now became not only productive, but fun, too. I quickly learned that the fishing items I was importing from Taiwan I could easily sell to local stores at a big discount. You see, stores bought from wholesalers, wholesalers bought from distributors, distributors from importers, importers from exporters, exporters from manufacturers. Sometimes I found the length of middlemen to be ridiculously long. Every step I traced resulted in a cheaper price for the item. By the time you get to the manufacturer, the price isn't a half, a quarter or a tenth of the market price, but a tiny fraction. I thought the whole thing was exciting. And I couldn't deny there was a fortune to be made.

So I kept up work at the office and learned some basics about the mail-order business from *Mark* along the way. After all, this was just a hobby, right? Letters and phone calls to foreign manufacturers produced price lists, catalogs, and samples. With the easily obtained materials, I had all I needed to construct advertising copy. I designed my own ads, using illustrations and photos of fishing products. I even joined a few fishing clubs, both locally and nationally, and began a few correspondences.

When I felt the time was right, I placed ads with *Outdoor Life, Field and Stream,* and *Popular Science* magazines. I began my mail order business from the garage. My home town's trade license was ten bucks and I had a letterhead made up for my company stationery and 1,000 return envelopes. Did it all myself with a little help from *Mark*. I photocopied product lists and prices with product descriptions. I made a complete list of everything I wanted to sell in the next 12 months.

I felt comfortable with the small risk. I still had my other job and only a small amount of money was actually invested in my business preparations and inventory. Through the starting stages of the business, my wife called my interest 'tinkering.' I was much happier with myself and my spare time. The shock, a happy one, came when I started getting orders so fast I sold through my inventory in half the anticipated time. But the profit margin from the manufacturers' market was so great that I bought twice as much in my second order. And still I didn't deplete my profit. The third time I bought, I ordered five times my conservative initial order. Still, the profit left after costs of merchandise and advertising (shipping and supplies, too) enabled me to buy more advertising space from more magazines.

All I did was keep up with the orders and expand with the profits. 'Success' was there before I even noticed. I made $425,000 in the first eleven months. Now my friends joke that I never have time to join them on our fishing trips. Not true. I still occasionally make a lure and tie a fly. In the small office that my business supports, I have other people to unpack supplies, ship the orders, and stay in touch with the customers. Oh, and we branched out, too. The profit margin gives me enough money for bigger ads, so I've added fishing line, tackle boxes, knives, snakebite kits, you name it.

And 'spare time' caused all this in the first place. Oh, I still have some of that. I own a thriving business and I let other people take care of it when I'm away - 'gone fishin.' No, I still don't have a hobby. But I don't worry about that anymore.

A Sincere Thanks To My Good Friend *Mark J. Reynolds.*

Your friend,

C. A. Pierce
Clear Water, Florida

Chapter 1

STEP ONE

Start of The Magic Nine System!

By reading a few dozen American magazines you will no doubt be able to spot the "perfect" product to start the system with. You might wake up in the middle of the night and realize no one ever thought of selling a "such-and-such" before in *Popular Sicence Magazine.* Possibly you suddenly thought of a, fast-selling, always-wanted product and knew it was available only to you, from Taiwan, at an incredibly low, low price. Of course, you immediately went right out and bought ten jillion of them and set right out to make $10,000,000 million bucks. Well, you and I and just about everyone else knows it rarely happens that way and, while legends are sometimes born like that, most of the people who begin with the system trust in the nine basic steps to determine what they will sell and how they'll go about purchasing it.

Yes, there are basic steps for answering questions like what to sell and how to buy it. Not everyone invents a Frisbee or a Yo-Yo, we aren't all inventors or engineers, and we aren't all authorities on whats in-demand today. The reason the magic system has made so much money for so few people lies in the fact that a little research builds a strong foundation.

Many people know the old adage from the newspaper business: the five W's. "Who, What, Where, When, and Why—and some add How." Think of your own current situation this way. You are working for someone else, doing what you know how to do, working outside the home forty hours (or more) a week for a paycheck. You came into this situation because "that's the way it's done." But look at this a little more closely. In order to get that job, you had to sell yourself to a boss. When you got that job, you traded your abilities and your time for a paycheck. Simple enough. The company or your boss gets the profits. You're left with the work and a paycheck, little else. Oh, you also get the boss's demands and the drawbacks of others in trying to get your work done.

That can be a little depressing when you look at it so simply. "That's the way it's done," you say. But let's look at it a little differently and add a few new ingredients. If you want to change the outcome, isolate the Who, When, and Why. What you're concerned with is You, Now, and Money. Again, simple enough. It's the What and the How that stumps the imagination of most people. They look around, see "the way it's done," and assume the only answer is working somewhere for someone else and doing something that's needed in trade for the paycheck.

But what can you sell that isn't pigeon-holed labor that anyone can do? If you answer the What and How with the concept of home-based mail order, the outcome changes. But you need specifics. Bear in mind the five W's (and H) as you go through the basic steps of discovering what to sell and how to find it. The other W's will become You, Now, From Home, and For Profit.

The "What" to sell can appear to be an immense question when asked alone and in the dark. All things sold in a mail order business can be sold right from your own kitchen table. They are either items of merchandise or information. All merchandise or information must be of general consumer use. As you approach your mail order business, keep those guidelines in mind.

Anything can be sold through mail order but some things are better than others. Some things are ideal. If you are considering merchandise (products from the Far East), avoid items that are too bulky or heavy. Ask yourself if the item is fragile or spoils quickly or easily. Will it require lots of testing and experience, does it require low risk, is it a good "starter" item for a business that has a plan for expansion?

From your experience you may want to sell something you are familiar with or something you enjoy. Ask yourself, ask around, read the advertising copy in every *Old* magazine you can get your hands on. What do people want? What are people needing and finding hard to obtain. If you're answering those questions with a item that is sold in every retail store from coast to coast, remember that you'll have a lot of competition from that market and you may not be able to buy it cheap enough to sell it at a large profit. You might do better with an item that is unusual in some way, or unique. Perhaps it's hard to get or distinctive in nature. If you have an idea in mind, ask yourself if other items are related to it. Later, after the single item has proven itself, you'll want to add other items to your inventory to develop the related line of items so your business expands. One shot deals have a way of running their course, so don't limit the potential of your business right from the start.

Something as simple as the phone book can get the imagination started. Go through the Yellow Pages. There's no end to the things people need if the phone book is any proof. Still without a thought? Another obvious and available source of ideas is the library. Ask for old magazines. Even if you know what you will be selling, you'll want to use these sources anyway to see if someone sold the item two or three years ago. The phone book will give you names and addresses for retail stores, distributors, and wholesalers. It will give you a wide picture of generalized, specialty, and related merchandise. You're going to be writing letters, making phone calls, getting catalogs, and thumbing brochures. You're going to start getting to know the waters and no longer "just thinking about it."

Part of your "What" and "How" will run together and be your first steps. Two excellent directories for imported items are *Made in Europe* and *Hong Kong Enterprise.* (I have listed their addresses in the back of this volume.) When you proceed with an imported item, you'll need to understand your flow of orders in order to keep inventories ready for quick shipping. Also, read a few good European newspapers frequently and be on the look-out for new products or emerging markets. *Direct Marketing Magazine,* produced especially for your interests, can offer you several mail order sales counselors, for whose services you'll have to pay, but a wealth of information as well as marketability suggestions can be yours for little cost by subscribing to *Direct Marketing Magazine.*

When you begin to zero in on the kind of merchandise you will be selling, subscribe to the various trade journals produced by that market. See what's offered, who offers it, what's new and different. Attending a generalized or specific products trade show can open dozens of doors to both your imagination and information needs. Once you have collected specific manufacturers names and addresses, you'll begin with letters of inquiry, followed by a telex call.

As you begin to answer the question of What to sell and Who to buy it from, consider the question of How much it's going to cost. You'll want an item with a long profit margin, anywhere from 100 percent to 2,000 percent. You will have the expenses of the product itself and its advertisements to consider as well as the cost of direct mail materials and back-end promotional literature. You must be able to sell it at a cost to customers that covers those known expenses, so don't pay too much for a product and then sell it too cheaply just to have a price edge on your competition. You don't have to ask your customers to pay too much, but you DO have to pay as little as possible yourself. So don't go with the first manufacturer you find. Keep writing letters to more and more. A little digging will pay off in big profits to you.

You'll find that some items are franchised to agreed upon retail outlets at agreed upon costs and prices. Yet more and more importers and manufacturers are beginning to sell direct. The number of middlemen, wholesalers, jobbers, and distributors, you can eliminate will mean a greater share in mark-up profits that are yours to start with. Direct sellers' prices usually begin less than the wholesale price and fractions of the retail price. When an item is available from an overseas market, particularly the far east, a quality, handsome wrist watch which sells for two hundred dollars at the established department store can cost, when bought in quantity, as little as nine dollars.

If you are considering the "gimmicks and gadgets" market, an excellent source for ideas on specifics might be the *Taiwan Products Guidance Magazine- 5 Chung 12th Road-P.O. Box 68-855- Taipei, Taiwan, R.O.C.* The Clearinghouse for New "Gimmicks and Gadgets"and they can put you on their mailing list to receive comprehensive reports on many manufacturing industries, plastic products, kitchen instruments, furniture, toys—the list of product ideas and availabilities is nearly endless.

Consider your next step once you've identified an item for your business and a list of product sources. You will be writing to manufacturers and distributors. It would be important at this point to consider professional and attractive looking letterhead stationery for your inquiry. Your inquiries should be typed, not handwritten. In a clear, straight forward manner, be specific about your request for samples, catalog and brochure, and/or price list. Include only pertinent information, keep it neat, organized, brief, and to the point. Offer to pay in advance or inquire about their payment arrangements. This will facilitate your requests, terms, and speed your orders. "Open accounts" may not be offered or will only delay matters while a time consuming credit check is run on your company's account with your bank. Include a business card as well, if you have one. The more professional you appear to be with that first letter of inquiry, the more likely you are to receive prompt and serious consideration.

If you're still at a loss for merchandise to sell, look for give-aways, liquidations, or going-out-of-business notices. Good ideas might be old ideas re-cycled. While going through old magazines. You may find an old idea whose time has come around again. We've all heard how young people have more money to spend than their parents, so stay in touch with kids, see what their interests are, what hobby the generation is into, listen to what they have to say about their needs and wants. Be observant. Spot trends.

While handling merchandise may be up your alley or in tune with your experience and interests, not all mail order businesses concern themselves with products and goods bought from the off shore manufacturing market. The second and perhaps the most growing field of sales is information. (Books) In our Information Age, individuals, groups, and businesses are hungry for information on an unlimited array of topics. People enjoy information that shows them how to do something, how to make an item that interests and pleases them, and how to learn through manuals, books, courses, and sharing information through newsletters.

This is perhaps the easiest end of mail order to get into. It entails little cost, except for paper and printing, and it doesn't have to involve volumes of pages, yet the successful information business must be of high quality and usefulness. Unlike merchandise mail order, information mail order doesn't require large storage space or risk breakage and spoilage. Also, the book rate for mailing information is the least expensive route for shipping.

It might be that everything you need to sell to your customers is already in your head. You may have experience in a number of fields that other working people don't have yet due to your maturity and knowledge of related fields. If you choose a topic of your knowledge, structure it on paper and expand it with a book or manual. Waves of popular information create a powerful coattail effect and you should start as soon as possible to get in on the demand.

Study the information market and the ripeness will be readily apparent. There are countless "always-in-demand" book topics such as how to lose weight, how to become more healthy or beautiful by exercising. Instruction information abounds with how to make more money, build a better birdhouse, fix a car or TV, or how to sew, paint, do odd-jobs around the house. People are always interested in how to make friends, use a computer, play a better game of tennis, or play a musical instrument. Just what information you choose to sell will require a study of the market. It can be a twenty-five page booklet on how to save time doing the housework or a ten page piece on how to run a successful yardsale. Again, it's not the number of pages that counts, but the quality of the information. Does it provide a valuable service or will the knowledge be financially rewarding?

Your finished product should be put in the hands of a quality printer or can be professionally produced even by some local printers.You should strive for an attractive appearance and it should be easy to read. You could network related topics, thus expand your "line of goods" or develop a series of related information publications.

You've heard of seminars that can cost hundreds of dollars to attend. That demonstrates that people need and want information. Think how many more people would willingly skip the expensive seminar for information that sells for ten or twenty dollars. Perhaps you've operated a business before or worked in a store. People want to know how to begin a retail operation, set up a warehouse, organize displays, or keep records. Everyone owns cookbooks and you may have or be able to organize recipes on quick dinners, impressive desserts, or how to bake a perfect loaf of bread.

One of the hottest information aids on the market in recent years is that which helps people get a job, how to have a successful interview, or write a winning resume. If the preceding decade was called "The Me Generation," this current generation can well be called the "How-To" generation. But always keep in mind, that your information business should be geared to the gereral consumer.

Many of the same resources for finding an item of merchandise to sell will also yield designated customers for the information you sell. Identify your market and find out what it is they want to know. A simple talent for research and organization of ideas will produce an information book you can sell. Newsletters and updates on businesses often contain a simple compilation of existing and breaking news. New interests across the country are spread because people want to know something about something or how to do it. Even the old stand-bys of instruction in a craft or ideas for a project can be relied on. What you know or can find out can be passed on to others through a little ingenuity on your part because the thirst for information is never quenched.

Now that you see that the "What" and "How" of our original question can be answered, where do you go from here? With diligence and guidance from these sources, a step-by-step forward effort is all it takes. Be it products from

Taiwan or books from your own mind, select the right item for the right medium. It may be a luxury or a necessity, it may be electronic or instructional, or it may be generalized or seasonal. It all works on its own level and in its own way. The only thing lacking is action by you.

The **"Millionaire Bus"** Is Starting To Pick Up Speed.

Chapter Two

STEP TWO
Important Information About the Countries You Will Be Importing Products From.

Note! The following information in this chapter is the most important part of the first program. *It is very significant that you fully understand the people and the countries you will be dealing with, and the various ways of negotiation. Please read it carefully. I think you will find it extremely informative and potentially entertaining.*

Selling exotic products imported from foreign lands is an exciting way to make money. The initial investment need not be great but can be whatever makes you comfortable. If you already are mechanically inclined you might want to market tools in metric or English measurements. Or if you like linens, lace and embroideries you will concentrate your efforts in different countries where these are produced at good export prices. We will discuss how to select products and how to sell them.

When you are the buyer, you are an American importer. Your source is the foreign seller, the exporter. In this chapter, your international business, prices and monetary values will be expressed in the local currency, exactly the way the exporter, your supplier, will quote prices to you. Sometimes the prices will be quoted in United States dollars: US$ 35.75. Dollars come from more than one country, just like francs come from France, Switzerland, Belgium and other countries, and each one has a different value or exchange rate with your dollar, whether your dollar is from the United States, Canada or Hong Kong.

Dollars can be expressed US$ 35.75, C$ 35.75 or HK$ 35.75. In early 1986, C$ 35.75 was equal to US$ 25.03; and HK$ 35.75 was worth US$ 4.58. In other words, the Canadian dollar was worth .70 US¢ and the Hong Kong dollar was worth .13 US¢. Normally French Francs are expressed 20 500 FF 42; twenty thousand five hundred French francs and 42 centimes. Sometimes the same value can be written FF 20.500,42.

Whether the foreigners switch periods and commas around should not alarm you. In the end it will make sense and you will handle the differences easily.

Most large American newspapers carry a daily exchange rate column in the business or financial section. In that column the major currencies of the world are compared to the United States dollar. If you are travelling abroad you will still find the same type of exchange-column. Just remember, the currencies will probably be compared to the local currency!

WHICH COMES FIRST?

Would you like to import products from Hong Kong, or Singapore, or Korea? Japan? Taiwan? Tahiti?

Would you like to distribute a full set of steel metric tools that retails for $ 39.99 at your hardware store, - but you can buy the set for $12.00 in Hong Kong? In United States dollars, that is.

Is there an export duty?

Is the product on the embargo list? Does the country of origin have an agreement with your country to prevent its export? Does your country prevent its import?

Is there an import duty? There usually is.

The answers are simple enough to determine. The State Department can usually supply information about any country you are interested it. Your local librarian can do the same and probably better. If you telephone a desk officer at the State Department you will not be given a great deal of time and you will be transferred to a public relations person. This person will know less about what you need than any good librarian.

Most foreign countries maintain consulates in major American cities. They will always have up-to-date and useful brochures and newsletters for you. This is the best place to start asking for the names of trade organizations in their countries. Those trade groups will have many names of suppliers of the type of product you might want to import.

You should remember that the product you may be interested in importing is probably manufacturered in only a few countries. On the other hand, if you want to handle goods from a specific country or geographic area, your search should be concentrated on a line of allied goods.

Imagine that in addition to your mail order business that you want to be a wholesaler-importer for your local area. Your local customers may be gift shops and that there are 200 to 300 gift shops within a given two hundred mile area. If you are to supplement your mail order business with local sales, you will want to have products that are normally sold in gift shops. If your business will be strictly mail order, then you will want storage space and a minimum of repackaging to ship to your customers.

The type of packaging you receive will help to determine your cost of repackaging and shipping. You will have to inspect completely or by statistical sampling of the goods you receive from abroad.

It is this type of information that you will gather when you perform your market and product studies.

If you import crystal glassware, you will have to inspect each piece for breakage or chipping. Obviously, you may have increased insurance costs because of the high risk. This may be offset by the reliability of the exporter who may excell in safe packaging and the insurance companies know the exporter's reputation.

The situation is completely reversed if you are importing stainless steel wrench sets.

Usually prices for export will be quoted as CIF or FAS. These initials are understood everywhere. The CIF price includes cost of the product, the cost of insurance, and the cost of the prepaid freight charges. The FAS price means the cost of the goods and the packaging laying *along side* the ship; this means waiting to be put on a carrier, whether a ship or an airplane. You must arrange the insurance and the delivery yourself or hire a local export broker to do it.

If you pay US$ 18.00 per item for the product CIF and your local handling cost is $2.40, you will gross 40% if you sell it to a retailer for $28.56 and he will sell it for $ 39.99 to make his 40%. In this case you are acting as a distributor or wholesaler. If you mail order the item for $39.99 you will earn nearly 100%. Example:

Cost of product abroad	$ 12.00
Insurance	2.00
Freight	4.00
CIF	18.00
Import tax & Local handling	2.40
Subtotal	20.40
40% profit	8.16
Selling Price	$ 28.56

In the example above, if you sell 100 items to one store, your profit would be $810.60. If you sold one item each to 100 different mail order customers you would earn a profit of $1,950.50 less the cost of advertising.

Since the customer pays the cost of freight or mailing, these costs are not shown because they do not affect the profit line in the example.

PICKING A MODEL GEOGRAPHIC AREA

The British Crown Colony of Hong Kong will be used as an example in depth as a typical exporting country. A very broad range of products is exported from Hong Kong. Many products are produced or manufactured there. A large number of products are imported and warehoused in Hong Kong and exported to third countries. The re-exported-products are usually from mainland China, the People's Republic of China.

There is not enough room in this entire book, *"America's Fastest Way To Become A Millionaire"* to explore each exporting country in detail. Hong Kong is an excellent example because of the aggressive exporting policies of its government and its businessmen and of its centralized location, geographically and financially. Japan, Korea, and Taiwan are to its north. Singapore, Philippines, and Australia are to the south and southeast. China is in its back yard. In 1997 Hong Kong will revert to China, the most populated country in the world, and the country the most anxious to earn hard currency. There is no harder currency that the United States dollar.

Hong Kong has always been a key gateway to the Orient. Some of the world's best businessmen are there. There are virtually no export taxes or regulations on any legal product or manufactured goods.

INTRODUCTION TO HONG KONG

Hong Kong enjoys the reputation of having one of the most beautiful harbors in the world...and even more spectacular at night. The colony is about half the size of the state of Rhode Island. There are about 5,400,000 people living in these 410 square miles. Most of the population is Chinese and slightly more than half are in the work force.

No one visiting Hong Kong can fail to be impressed by its vitality. In addition to being the third financial center in the world, it has earned an international reputation as a leading manufacturing and commercial center. Hong Kong arose from the determination of Britain's merchant adventurers to establish a permanent foothold for their commerce with China. British sailing ships supported the mercantile community at the place people considered a "barren rock" when a Royal Navy officer planted the flag there in 1841.

The island thrived under the British and it soon became the focal point of Chinese emigration from the mainland. Attracted by the new opportunities, settlers flooded into Hong Kong from China.

Like Hawaii which is made up of many islands but only one named Hawaii, there is one island named Hong Kong but there are many islands and a peninsula that constitute the Colony of Hong Kong.

The Convention of Peking in October 1860 added to Hong Kong Island's 29 square miles another 3.6 square miles by ceding Kowloon peninsula and Stonecutters Island. Later, China leased to Britain the 371 square miles of land next to Kowloon in 1898. This is the lease that expires on June 30, 1997. Successive reclamations have brought the colony to its present 410 square miles.

On December 19, 1984 Britain and China ratified a joint declaration returning all of the colony to China in 1997. China agreed to administer the colony with a high degree of autonomy as a Special Administrative Region. China is expected to exploit this jewel of the orient as Hong Kong will probably be China's greatest asset to earn hard currency.

Hong Kong's prosperity revolved around its harbor, whose anchorage of 14,800 acres is among the finest in the world. In Hong Kong, as in the rest of the orient, the metric system is used almost exclusively. There, the anchorage would be described as having 6,000 hectares.

The port was selected for sailing ships like the swift tea clippers. Today the harbor caters for all types of modern vessels, from containers ships and bulk carriers to cargo vessels, tankers and passenger liners.

The population densities in several areas of the colony are unmatched anywhere in Asia. The built-up areas of Hong Kong Island and New Kowloon average up to 165,000 to the square kilometer, or 427,350 per square mile.

The core of Hong Kong's communications, the keypoint of sea and air routes through Asia, continues to be located in the harbor. The seaport, airport and rail terminals are within a radius of three miles. More than 22,000 ocean-going vessels enter and clear the port annually, discharging or loading over 37 million tons of cargo. The container terminal, situated at Kwai Chung, is the third largest in the world. Thirty-two airlines operate over 900 scheduled flights a week to help move 7,300,000 passengers annually. Air cargo exceeds 300,000 tons a year.

Coupled to the communications and transport capabilities to support virtually any volume of exports, any important element to consider is the excellent telecommunications links to Hong Kong.

Anyone who is considering an entry into the import and export trade must consider the importance of communications in bringing a negotiation to a successful conclusion, or to put final details on shipping instructions for key supplies needed for a holiday promotion and sale.

In the case of Hong Kong, there are several earth terminals for satellite communications. In addition to telephone circuits, there are telex and telegram services as well as telephotocopying at high speed. There are satellite connections with over 30 countries. An 80-channel submarine coaxial cable links the colony with Malaysia, Singapore and the U.S. possession Guam, while another, with 1840 circuits, links Luzon in the Philippines and Okinawa.

These circuits connect with other cable systems to the United States, Canada, Japan, Australia and the entire asian and southeast asian network. Hong Kong residents can direct-distance-dial to more than 100 countries.

For Hong Kong's first 100 years the colony served as a warehouse for other people's products. China was both a supplier and a consumer. World War II and the Japanese occupation was an unhappy period during which everyone reflected on the future and the past. When the British resumed control in 1945 there was a concensus that there would no longer be business as usual.

When mainland China went communist, the colony's traditional market evaporated in 1951. The colonists had no choice but to develop manufacturing skills. For years Hong Kong, like Japan, became known as a copycat; imitating the products of other countries, producing them with cheap labor, and dumping lots of cheap goods on any market that would accept them.

However, cheap labor was the key then and is the key now. If everything else is the same; that is, the cost of materials are the same and the cost of shipment is the same, then the goods produced in the country with the cheapest labor is the best place for an importer to buy.

There is more than the cost of labor involved. But the importer, the buyer, should know that these factors will influence the prices of goods that are being sold overseas.

It is because of the cheap labor in Hong Kong that high-fashion designers set up garment factories in the colony. When high fashion designers expanded into the ready-to-wear business, they flocked to areas where skilled and inexpensive labor produced the fine garments that retail stores wanted.

HOW TO START LOOKING FOR THE RIGHT PRODUCT TO IMPORT AT THE RIGHT PRICE

The best way to start is at the beginning. There are letters to write. While you are waiting for the replies, go to the local library with a pad and pen to take notes.

Places to write to in the United States and Canada are:

British Embassy - Hong Kong Office
3100 Massachusetts Avenue, N.W.
Washington, D.C. 20008

Industrial Promotion Office of Hong Kong
McKesson Plaza Building   Suite 2130
1 Post Street
San Francisco, California 94104

Hong Kong Trade Development Council
333 North Michigan Avenue   Suite 2028
Chicago, Illinois 60601

Hong Kong Trade Development Council
154-2 World Trade Center
2050 Stemmons Freeway
Dallas, Texas 75258

Hong Kong Trade Development Council
Suite 1100 National Building
347 Bay Street
Toronto, Ont. M5H 2R7 Canada

Office of the Commissioner for
   Hong Kong Commercial Affairs
British Consulate General
Tower 56 17/F
126 East 56 Street
New York, New York 10022

The business of Hong Kong, people there are proud to say, is business. There are over 600 American firms with offices in Hong Kong. Thousands more are doing business through local agents and distributors. Almost anywhere in the world you will find a Chamber of Commerce. In Hong Kong it is:

The American Chamber of Commerce in Hong Kong
1030 Swire House
HONG KONG   Telephone: 5-260165

You will almost always find an American Embassy or an American Consulate to help you. Here, it is:

Foreign Commercial Service
American Consulate General
26 Garden Road
Hong Kong

The American Chamber of Commerce in Hong Kong is a member of the APCAC - the Asia Pacific Council of American Chambers of Commerce. In addition, they will sell you an up-to-date compendium of information called *DOING BUSINESS IN TODAY'S HONG KONG*. They are also looking ahead to the huge trade possibilities with mainland China and are offering a book called *DOING BUSINESS IN TODAY'S CHINA*.

Usually the local United States Embassy or the appropriate desk officer at the State Department will be able to get you some key addresses to get started in your search for foreign suppliers. Do not rely on the United States agencies to get you precise names of foreign sellers or for commercial advice about the fairness of prices being quoted to you.

The American representatives will refer you to competent foreign agencies who represent the foreign sellers and occasionally will refer you to people engaged in providing services or financial reports. They may also let you know which American banks have local branches in the foreign city you may be interested in.

Usually your own local banker will have a list of banks with which your own bank has corresponding relations. These corresponding banks may be among the largest in the world, perhaps with a branch in Hong Kong.

Therefore, your neighborhood banker, who may also be your loan officer, can give you a few addresses abroad and in Hong Kong. By writing directly to a bank there, you can get some good trade information on specific suppliers and on current regulations or restrictions, if any.

There are over one hundred branch offices of foreign banks operating in Hong Kong. Many of these are American banks. Just about every large bank in every state of the union has a corresponding bank in Hong Kong and may well be associated with one of the 128 licensed Hong Kong banks. There are over 1,500 banking offices spread throughout the colony. No one has trouble finding a bank in Hong Kong.

Local Hong Kong banks are regulated by the office of the British Commissioner of Banking, who is also the Commissioner of Deposit-taking Companies. A Hong Kong bank cannot get a charter without having at least US$13,800,000 in paid-up capital. In Hong Kong Dollars this amount is HK$100,000,000. Actually, by U.S. standards this is not a great deal of strength. You might be better off dealing with an American bank that corresponds with your own.

Hong Kong manufactures clothing, textiles, electronics, plastic products, toys, watches, and clocks. These constitute about three-quarters of all the exports from Hong Kong to various places in the world. The biggest export segment is in textiles and clothing.

There is a great deal of cotton yarn production and some blended cotton and man-made fibre production. In addition to yarn, there are knit products, fabrics, and then clothing. Available are all categories such as, fabrics for dyeing, screen printing, pre-shrinking, and permanent pressing. Many suppliers will be able to produce customized goods. An example of this would be customized screen-printed T-shirts.

Their electronics industry has been growing and Hong Kong manufacturers have been exporting integrated circuits, wafer chips for integrated circuits, electronic modules, semiconductors, liquid crystal displays, quartz crystals, multilayer printed circuit boards, computer memory systems, microcomputers and their components. Finished products have included calculators, radios, recorders, television sets, cordless telephones and telephones with built-in memories.

The colony is probably the world's largest supplier of toys. Since many toys now have battery-driven mechanisms and even electronic devices, there will be stronger relationship between the electronics industry and the toy industry.

Hong Kong also produces travel goods, handbags and similar products, metal products, jewellry, domestic electrical equipment, electrical machinery, apparatus and appliances, optical articles, and photographic goods.

When studying the possibilities of importing electrical goods, bear in mind that virtually all consumer products in the United States operate on 110 volts. Most foreign electrical goods for consumers operate on 220 volts. Even the amperage is different. Insist on technical specifications very carefully.

Metrication is also an important feature. Metrication? Sounds like a medicine. This is the use of metric measures. The word is often used to indicate that a country is changing from the use of English measure to metric measure. One meter is equal to 3.28 feet. One kilometer is a little more than a half-mile. A liter is more than one quart. A kilogram, usually called a kilo, is 2.2 pounds.

Often an ordinary pocket dictionary will have a simple conversion table near the word "Measure," and many daily calendars used to keep appointments often have a conversion table. If you want to import, have a conversion table handy.

It will not take a person long to get information on any country from which you may want to import. Yet, you must compare sources. If you want to import canned food, Hong Kong will not be the first place to look. Hong Kong imports much of its food and cannot yet feed itself. Yet, nearby are many suppliers in Taiwan, with exports like pineapples, mushrooms, asparagus; as well as volume items like sugar, rice and bananas.

We will discuss Taiwan, Republic of China, separately. It is a different country altogether, and has no connection politically and commercially with either Hong Kong or The People's Republic of China.

The People's Republic of China has a vital link with Hong Kong and will take the colony over in 1997 as we have described earlier.

Hong Kong is stable. It has been stable under the rule of the United Kingdom. It is apt to be stable under the Chinese. But there is no guarantee. History has shown some developing countries to be very unstable, subject to political upheavals and revolts. All the normal stability factors indicate that a Hong Kong supplier should not have any problems being a reliable supplier to an American importer for many years to come.

Once you have narrowed down the number of potential sources of a product that interests you to import, you will want to examine the specifications and the prices carefully.

PRICES, TERMS AND RELIABILITY

Price is a major consideration in selecting a supplier. It is, however, just one of many factors which will influence your decision to buy from one supplier rather than another.

One advantage in dealing with Hong Kong is the language. Most Chinese and other citizens of Hong Kong use English as their commercial language. Nonetheless, you may well run into an excellent supplier whose English is terrible! Or you may run into a supplier whose English is quite good but only pretends to have trouble writing or speaking it. This is true anywhere in the world.

Usually you will want to see a sample of a product. Let us use an example of a mantle clock. You have decided to mail order a clock with chimes on the hour. The manufacturer may have several chimes to offer and several types of wood finishes, and a choice of roman numerals, arabic numerals, or gold tacks instead of face-numbers. For marketing purposes you may have decided you only want to portray one single product without options to simplify storage, handling, and processing of the orders.

One of your major considerations will be uniformity of the products, reliability, good packaging, one single chime like Westminster, one type of clock-face. If your supplier is the manufacturer and he will produce the whole order, there should be a better chance all the products will be the same, than would be the case if your supplier is a dealer and has four manufacturers producing the model you want.

There is always a second side to the coin in business. If your single supplier decides to go on a month's vacation or on a permanent vacation in the middle of your mail order campaign he would leave you high and dry when you need it least! If you were buying from a dealer with four producers then you would not suffer if one producer failed or closed or changed its product line. The use of the dealer would give you some protection, but it would probably cost you an extra 15%.

In many aspects, you will want to eliminate the middle man to lower your costs. Bear in mind that you are a middle man, too! There are always middle men between the manufacturer and the consumer! There are always middle men between the farmer and the consumer!

There are good reasons for cooperatives, trade organizations, distributors, wholesalers, jobbers, and brokers. You have a strong interest in dealing directly with a reliable manufacturer or with two reliable manufacturers. Each case differs.

Much will depend on whether you want to handle a single product for your mail order business, or just a few products that can be sold through one ad. If you want to sell through a catalog, then you may have to develop a line of similar goods or an interesting assortment of various types to attract more people.

Consequently, if you want to develop a line of products or a variety of products, you may have no other choice but to deal with an agent or a foreign dealer. Sometimes a dealer can bring an unusual opportunity if a manufacturer is closing out a line and is willing to sell at half the market price to avoid keeping the products in inventory. There are no set rules. My purpose here is to outline as many scenarios as possible to alert you to situations to watch for.

Costs may vary with volume and frequency of purchases. If you buy 50 items monthly, you will not have the same price and terms as some competitor who is buying 5000 a week from the same supplier. Another very critical factor is the "delay in delivery." This term relates to the time it takes for a supplier to deliver the goods to you once he has received a firm order. An exporter will want a firm, irrevocable order, plus the assurance he will be paid. All exporters want to be paid in advance. Why not, wouldn't you? It is better to work out terms that protect you. We will discuss this separately.

A manufcturer will break his neck to satisfy the 5000-item-per-week-buyer, even if it means losing you as a customer. However, if he has to wait for his money with the bigger buyer, he may make an exception for you since he will be paid the same day if you worked out that type of payment terms.

FORGET POLITICS AND GO FOR THE ACTION

Unless you absolutely want to deal with a certain country, i.e., Korea because you understand Korean; Macao because you speak Portuguese, or Tahiti because you speak French, then conduct the market search on the basis of the best product at the best price and terms from a reliable supplier. Forget the supplier's politics and forget his religion or what have you.

As you forget politics, do not forget logic. You might fall in love with certain hand-embroidered tablecloths from a communist country that may have a track record of breaking off relations with countries, especially the U.S.A. Then you might want to think twice about relying on a supplier in that country even if the supplier is not a member of the communist party. He may not be, but his Board of Directors is.

You may not lose your money but you may have lost a selling season.

In the case of Hong Kong, it will remain reliable for at least a decade and there is every reason to believe that mainland China will keep the territory reliable because China needs hard currency earnings desperately.

Moreover China may be harder on malefactors and cheaters than has been Britain. Any country that still executes thieves in the village square to set a good example will probably insist on honest business dealings, as is the case in China.

Anyone who investigates the Hong Kong market should sample the mainland Chinese possibilities at the same time. The economic section of the Chinese Embassy in Washington should be able to help:

Economic Section
Embassy of the People's Republic of China
2300 Connecticut Avenue, N.W.
Washington, D.C. 20008

As in almost all communist countries, there are collectives representing the export trade. There has been some loosening of these rigid guidelines in the domestic trade. It is possible that some independent traders may exist in the future. For the forseeable future, anyone interested in importing goods suitable for consumer mail ordering will have to write to organizations like the following:

China National Cereals, Oil and Foodstuffs
   Import & Export Corp.
82 Donganmen Street
Beijing, People's Republic of China

The best procedure is to indicate to the Embassy what type of product you are interested in. You will not find electronic instruments, optical devices, and state-of-the-art equipment. However, you might find exquisite porcelain, glassware, beautiful embroideries, silks, carved wood chests, and most any type of article that is labor-intense. Almost any product whose main value is derived by man's careful labor and not by machine or assemblyline efficiency is a good item to search for in China.

The Chinese Embassy could put you in contact through an English-speaking official with a village of artisans in remote China that you would otherwise never find.

Just be polite. Be persistent. Be careful. Be patient. China probably has more good deals waiting to happen than any other supply market in the world. Be imaginative. The Chinese are new at this but look how fast they caught on in Hong Kong. At the outet, you will have no choice but to go through political channels to reach the right contact. You do not have to like the system to make it work but it can work, it does work. Make it work for you. Politics is the middleman in this case.

RECOGNIZING THE MIDDLEMAN

Sometimes it is impossible to recognize a middleman by his stationery or his letterhead. Some agents are also traders and will actually classify you by your inquiry, sending you a price list that differs from one he might send to another buyer.

Do not fear asking tough questions. Are you a manufacturer? Are you a jobber? Are you a manufacturer's agent? Do you represent a trading organization? Your supplier may be trying to get commissions from both ends. There is nothing wrong with it but you should try to determine it and perhaps avoid it if your instincts make you uncomfortable.

Some traders actually buy on their own account and maintain elaborate sales rooms in Hong Kong and sometimes in the United States or at international fairs. Many of their goods may be on consignment or they may buy only samples to show. If they are using samples, normally they have firm agreements with the manufacturers to supply the articles at a firm price, and at a reliable delivery rate and delay.

If you travel to Hong Kong, then you will arrange ahead of time to visit as many traders as possible. By viewing their wares and learning their prices and terms, you will soon have the flavor of values. Even if you never see the same articles later while visiting manufacturers, you will have a "sense" of what a good price is.

The first time you make a "sourcing" trip, it is worth the investment to hire or pay for whatever it takes to do it right. The American Chamber of Commerce in Hong Kong, with only a few weeks notice, can help organize introductions for you. The Hong Kong offices in the United States will help you as well. Always make an effort to contact the primary manufacturer as well as a trader or wholesaler. Each has his advantages. Give each of them the chance to show you what the advantages are.

You do not have to travel to secure a source. It is an option. You can do quite well and be successful without leaving the country. Taking an expensive business trip is not a guarantee of success. It ought to help. But the amount of homework and correspondence will still be the same. Everything must still be confirmed in writing.

Some agents are manufacturer's agents which is nothing more than a corporate sales representative in the U.S.A. The agent represents one manufacturer or a group of manufacturers through a trading company owned by the manufacturers. The agent usually is paid by the seller.

The question often arises, "Should I have a buying agent overseas?" People who have been in international trade for years sometimes use the telephone bill as the tool to decide this question.

Once your monthly telephone bill to one foreign city is equal to the round trip airfare, then you should have made the trip. If the monthly cost of airfares is equal to the monthly fee of a good agent, you should retain a local agent to represent your interests. No one has ever said this was the gospel truth. But it is an axiom followed by many experienced businessmen.

TERMS. MANY ARE NEGOTIABLE. MANY ARE NOT.

Once you have decided to buy a few samples of a product, you should press hard on the issue of terms as well as price and discounts. Whether you are buying through a manufacturer or through a trader or agent, you should hit on these matters at the beginning. The manufacturer has far more latitude than anyone else at the source to offer discounts. Consequently, you should look at competing products offered by other manufacturers and by traders and brokers.

Unless a manufacturer has a product so unique or so very superior to anything else, he ought to be able to offer substantial discounts below anything a trader or broker can offer.

However, you may not be able to meet the minimum order requirements of a manufacturer, a minimum order that a trader or broker could well ignore. Some manufacturers will do everything to help you except sell directly to you. Perhaps the manufacturer is too small to maintain a sales or exporting organization. Perhaps he has a licensing agreement which prevents him from selling into your market area. Ask. Ask why. Ask why not.

Are prices CIF? Sometimes an exporter is so familiar with his product and your own market that he quotes a fixed CIF price to you. If there are so many of these products in your area, you might want to forget this item and look for something else. The buyer usually pays for the insurance and the freight just as is the case in the U.S.A. Packaging is normally included in the sales price. It should be packed for export. The seller should know what is required to get it to you safely. Shipping by ship is cheaper than by air. The difference in arrival could be four to eight weeks. If you can afford the wait, shipment by sea will save you money. If not, you have no other choice but to pay the premium by air.

Get the best price you can consistent with the quality of the product. Be precise in specifying the details of the product. Even the color red is not specific. Try to assign a dye number or get swatches of the cloth or something painted with the red you have selected. Have the manufacture co-sign the specifications. Also, use specifications that can be checked or verified. If you say the vase must be lovely and attractive, you have lost because these are not specifications, these are adjectives which, at best, are still argumentative.

When importing you will have to give assurance that the supplier will be paid. A good commercial rating is fine, a good reputation is a must, and your best intentions are admirable. Until you demonstrate the willingness to pay and the readiness to do so, your selections will never be shipped to you.

There is always cash-in-advance. This is dangerous because if anything goes wrong or if the goods you receive are not what you wanted, nothing short of a war or a monumental law case will ever get your money back, and even then, probably will not. On a small sample order, it might be worth the risk just to determine if the supplier is such a shylock that he will cheat on a sample order. This is probably a safe situation given the alternatives and the time constraints to get a sample.

LETTER OF CREDIT

A letter of credit is a common instrument that your local banker can help you with. The supplier will insist on an irrevocable letter of credit. The supplier will tell you which bank is his and what his account number is with his bank. Upon his presentation of the invoice showing what he has packed and shipped to you, plus the receipt showing he has shipped them to you as agreed and with the proper insurance coverage, also properly receipted, the bank will pay him the cash. Normally, the goods he claims to have been shipped are in fact exactly as represented and everyone is happy. He has been paid. You have imported what you paid for.

The problem with this procedure is that you may have tied up good cash for a month or more. You should work out an arrangement with your bank to borrow the amount of the irrevocable letter-of-credit by use of a commitment. Pay the origination fee but do not borrow the money until it has been paid. Then pay it off as quickly as possible. If your banker is unwilling or unable to help you, try another bank.

CHECKING A SUPPLIER'S REPUTATION

This is one of the most difficult tasks to complete satisfactorily. The embassies, consulates, and official governmental bureaus normally cannot be involved in reporting on a business' reputation. Should the wrong word be said there will be serious consequences when the offended party reports the "offense" to his own government.

Even your bank will have difficulty. The "disclosure" laws, the slander laws, the right-to-privacy law, the "proprietary" rights doctrine of commercial law, all of these tend to make it very risky, and potentially very expensive for someone to say the wrong thing about a company.

There was a day when the American firm Dun and Bradstreet provided "ratings" that were accepted as the virtual word from on high. Other companies have ventured into this field. However, the accuracy and the timeliness of such ratings have diminished from the high levels of general acceptance of a generation ago. Such ratings are useful and if you can get one on a foreign supplier through these commercial organizations, do so.

These commercial reports differ from a consumer-credit report that is so easily generated in the United States. A Consumer credit report is an accepted intrusion into one's privacy in order to protect the lending organizations. There is no comparable commercial credit reporting system.

Most foreign organizations print the name and address of their bankers in the letterhead, plus the number of their account to make it easier for customers to pay directly bank to bank.

It is rare for an American company to disclose such information so readily. It is customary for most business bills to be settled by check and not by bank transfer or by wire. You will have to get familiar with payments by wire directly between banks. Almost every American bank is familiar with this and your bank will readily give you identification numbers and a special telephone number for you to use when you are ready.

If you have an employee stationed overseas he or she will report any useful information about a supplier routinely as you would have the right to expect. Learning such details from an agent who works for you and for other buyers will probably not happen, and it would be impractical for you to expect from an agent the level of frankness you would get from an employee.

Most people are tight-lipped about business affairs. This is very true overseas. Should you penetrate the veil of secrecy to obtain a credit report, how factual will it be? To begin with, most financial data in the report has been prepared by the supplier himself. He knows that it will be disclosed in the precise situation you are involved in—a credit check. What you will learn will be useful, but selective.

If the supplier has been in business for 50 years then that fact is important. If the company is new but the general manager has been in the business for many years and has recently left the other 50 year old company, there are good odds the new company will be a reliable supplier. Why? The general manager left a good job in a business he understands for a new position which he feels is a good prospect.

The supplier will normally give you background information. You can ask for a few references in English-speaking countries. You will probably get more information over the telephone than by letter. References in your locality may be self-defeating since they may be competitors of yours, or potential competitors. There is a certain language used between businessmen that is difficult to define. But one businessman recognizes it in another way—always. Use your telephone. Always ask your own bank to send an inquiry officially to its correspondent in the city of your supplier—in this case, Hong Kong.

The supplier expects you to do so and will not be surprised when his own bank reports the inquiry which *will* reach his bank. Many people claim that inter-bank credit checks are really no better than a courtesy call. They are worth more than that, at least there is a third party acknowledgement to your banker from someone he is aware of. Whatever information is passed on to you may be selective, inconclusive and incomplete, but it is worth something to you when added to other information you will develop on your own.

It is possible to get commercial credit reports on the executives of the company you want to check out. The fee is negotiable and will have to be paid up front. Usually the American Chamber of Commerce in a foreign city can provide the names and addresses of such organizations but will likely do so without any endorsement whatever.

You will be respected for being prudent and for searching prudently to acquire information on which to make an important business judgement. A credit check into the executives of a company can cut two ways. The credit service retained to do such a credit check could jeopardize your interests by disclosing your inquiry, thereby offending the foreign executives and possibly ruining any chance you had to do business with them and their company.

NEGOTIATIONS
"My word is my bond." How often have you heard that?
"His word is his bond." You would like people to say this about you.

This means you said you would do something and later did it. It does not mean you said you would do it and never took precautions to formalize your agreement.

Negotiations are often face to face and usually require a verbal exchange at some point with the use of a telephone. Sometimes, a negotiation can be conducted in writing but this takes longer.

The important thing is to confirm any agreement in writing.

The adage in business is: "Do not make a deal that cannot be reduced to writing, otherwise it is a bad deal." If you finally agree in a negotiation to accept an extra amount of articles in order to get a better price, agree on the language of the deal and agree for both parties to use the same language in a confirming letter. This is customary and is the fastest way to do things. Do not expect the supplier to rely on your word. That would be immature and impractical.

Your letter will help him in his business dealings with his own bank. The better your confirmation is the more easily he can acquire bank financing to produce the goods you want. He would rather have good bank financing than be forced to insist on terms that could scare you off, into the arms of his competitor. Once you have made your deal to your satisfaction, then it is in your best interests to give your supplier as many useful tools as you can to help him succeed.

Be as well prepared as you can be when the last round of bargaining occurs. The supplier will be, he may even have several assistants nearby to help him. Have all your own facts at your fingertips.

Whether you are in the last rounds of a negotiation or not, there are several points you should have listed on a memo pad to discuss to insure that both sides are starting from the same premises. For example, you should be prepared to discuss each of the headings below:

(1) The specifications of the product or articles you intend to order, the catalog numbers corresponding to each, and the model numbers or style numbers, the ranges and quantities of sizes, colors and any manufacturer's documentation that will help you with your own customers; and

1b) Any warranties or guarantees that the manufacturer will include, as well as allowances for breakage, spillage, or damage not directly attributable to the packing or the shipment; and

(c) The insurance coverage, by type and deductibles, and the extent of coverage; i.e., from the manufacturer's shipping room to your acceptance point; or only when the carrier actually takes possession at the ship's dock or once on the airplane; and

(d) If you do not intend to reopen and reseal the individual packages, will the manufacturer include your printed materials and, if so, will he print your text in Hong Kong, or will you have the printing done locally and you will ship the material to him in time to be included in the packing. If you are selling in the U.S.A. and in Canada, will you have French and Spanish language messages?

(e) Does your product require testing? Will the manufacturer certify in writing in a notice to be included in the original packing that it was tested and working properly immediately before packing?

(f) Markings. Depending on how many boxes or crates will be in a shipment, the markings you ask for are a critical part of the shipment and must be applied exactly as you have required in your instructions. These will be incorporated in the documentation normally accompanying a letter of credit (L/C). If there are six crates, you might want one numbered 1/6; the second 2/6; and up to 6/6, plus an "R" in eight-inch letters on at least three sides of the crate, with a three line address stenciled on the up side, or on the side with the printing to be read with the proper side up.

(g) Method of shipment and carrier. Usually the buyer indicates his choice of ocean shipment or air shipment and the arrival port of his convenience. The seller usually will arrange to ship it the way you have selected but will pick the local method to deliver to dockside or to the runway. There are no set rules and you may change the methods however you wish. Unless your request is outlandish, the seller will be pleased to accommodate your wishes. The costs of shipment will be passed on to you. The cost is estimated and sufficient funds will be included in the Letter-of-credit (L/C).

(h) Payment. We have already discussed payment in advance and the risk to you as the buyer. If a few hundred dollars are at stake for a few samples, you should take the risk if the supplier has checked out against your prudent inquiries. If the sample order is in the thousands of dollars, then you will want to use bankers even if only to work the kinks out of the pipeline.

It may be that you have been able to get an open account with 30, 60 or 90 day terms. For example, the supplier will ship at his expense and you will have 30 days to pay, or 60 days, or 90 days following the date of shipment. On their terms may be "Open, 4%/2% 60/net 90. This means you can take a 4% discount if you pay within 15 days of receiving the invoice, or take 2% discount if you pay between 16 and 60 days after; but that you must pay the invoice in full if you pay after the 60th day and you must pay before the 90th day.

Usually any L/C will be confirmed and irrevocable. Not many suppliers will accept any deal that is revocable which means you can cancel at any time without advance warning. This is like expecting your supplier to accept an order that can be cancelled without recourse, even after the items are in the manufacturing process.

Your bank is the issuing bank. Your supplier will consider this issuer an unconfirmed L/C if the issuing bank has no local branch in Hong Kong. The supplier will have to dispatch all the documentation to the bank and wait for payment by wire transfer to his local account. The only risk here is the potential loss of the original documents. Most suppliers will request a confirmed and irrevocable L/C, meaning that your bank will assign the paying responsibilities to a local Hong Kong bank.

The reason this aspect of international trade is more complex than the processing of orders within one's own country is the difficulty and near impossibility of successful litigation in a timely fashion. You do not want to have a law suit in Hong Kong. Your supplier does not want a law suit in North America.

It is at this time that the parties may face up to possible arguments and the possibility of accepting arbitration from organizations like The American Chamber of Commerce in Hong Kong or some other agreed upon international group acceptable to both sides in advance. By all means, try to tie down all the factors in writing to avoid any need for arbitration or litigation.

(i) How will you handle complaints from your customers who want their money back if the article arrives broken or different than you advertised? Will your supplier accept rejects and will you have to ship them back at your cost? If the incident of breakage is high your profits could be hurt. If you are handling delicate porcelains this is a very real consideration and the supplier of such articles should be well aware of your concerns. If you are importing tire irons, you ought to be able to get very favorable insurance rates and a risk-free distribution insofar as breakage is concerned.

(j) Inspection. When the shipments represent several thousand dollars you should consider inspections before packing and shipping. You may elect to go yourself the first time and show a local agent or banker what you expect for an inspection; i.e., a quick inspection at four design features on each item, or a very detailed inspection of all design features on every third article picked at random; or whatever fits the product or product line.

(k) Exclusivity. If you are purchasing only 5% of a producer's product line there is probably no chance he would agree not to supply the item to anyone else in North America. He might if you were importing to Bangladesh. But North America may represent 40% of his export market.

However, if your potential is high he may make a concession now and more later. If he understands that your orders could increase by 300% and his product does not have a great deal of competition yet, he may agree not to ship to other mail order firms for 12 months. Follow the golden rule. He with the gold will rule.

(l) Partial and late shipments. So long as you agree, the shipper may want to partial ship to help his cash flow. If this increases your per article cost you should negotiate a corresponding discount or reduction in your cost. Also, you should put a limitation on the number of partial shipments within a given time frame and you should limit the payment until everything has been shipped. For example, you may allow payment of 75% instead of 100%. This is not unusual, nor is it unfair. No experienced businessman would permit a 100% payment for a partial shipment. You need all your goods and the incentive will be there for the supplier to make good.

(m) Make-up of the invoice. You may be facing custom duties that are calculated on the total value of the imports. This is called *ad valorem*. This will include the basic purchase price, the insurance, the freight costs, and any incidental charge that is voucherable.

The U.S. Customs officer will probably have a duplicate-original of the invoice against which the bank will process the payment to your supplier. The officer is experienced and will recognize any effort to dilute the value of a product in order to pay less import duty.

If you have any broker's fees or agent's fees to pay as a function of invoice value, you should make provisions to pay and have the bank pay against a different invoice or formula that will not appear on the main invoice to avoid paying duty on an item that is not subject to duty. You are not avoiding a just duty, you will be avoiding an unpleasant argument.

Any factor that affects your landed costs or your ability to continue to maintain a profitable import mail order business is a factor to negotiate. In a very real sense your first order for samples is one which will shake out a great many details that will affect your complete landed cost. Your landed cost is not your total cost per article. You still have to pay for handling, inspection, transit losses, storage or warehousing, administrative costs for receiving and shipping, handling incoming orders, and shipping to your own customers, cost of advertising, and so forth. Your entire costs are divided by the number of articles to give you your actual cost.

A CLOSER LOOK AT HONG KONG AND ITS RELATIONSHIP WITH YOUR SUPPLIER

Hong Kong is essentially a free port and it collects revenue on only a few commodities: alcoholic liquors, tobacco, hydocarbon oils, cosmetics, non-alcoholic beverages and methyl alcohol. Import and export licensing is kept to a minimum and licenses are required only for dangerous drugs, strategic defense commodities, and textiles. Textiles is subject to international obligations. Some of the products controlled are obviously associated with health or security.

The Hong Kong Customs and Excise Service is responsible to collect revenue on dutiable commodities, for suppression of illegal traffic in narcotics and other prohibited goods and for the protection of copyrights. The service is a disciplined one and its officers are governed by special regulations. The service controls licenses for textiles and for issuing certificates of origin and trade declarations. It investigates trade complaints and enforces regulations on trade descriptions.

The Customs and Excise Service has three branches: Headquarters, Operations, and Investigation. The Service started in 1909 with only six Revenue Officers and 20 searchers. This has grown to a force of 2,700. The organization has changed to match its growing responsibilities. The Customs and Excise Officers will be found at all the import and export terminals in the colony.

Hong Kong International Airport, for example, is one where agents of the service will be found. It is one of the busiest in the world and the number of average daily passengers has grown to 12,000. Their baggage is inspected daily.

Officers are trained to avoid causing undue inconvenience to passengers. Baggage inspections are conducted on a selective basis. A total of 420,000 tons of cargo was handled at the air cargo complex in 1985. The service conducts occasional checks on exports but pays very close attention to articles entering the colony. This is achieved by an examination of import documents and of selected consignments arriving from narcotics-producing countries.

Over 23,000 ocean-going ships and 140,000 river trade vessels enter and leave Hong Kong's harbor each year. More than 12,000 files are kept in the service's ships files. Some of these ships are selected for a thorough search, normally conducted in mid-stream. These are searched by officers working in shifts around the clock. Although most ships receive only minimal attention from the customs inspectors, some ships may be guarded while in port to prevent any contraband from being landed. Cargo may be inspected on board or after off-landing.

Containerized cargo is discarged at the Kwai Chung Container Port. Officers at the port conduct occasional checks on export cargo and insure they are aware of all import cargo using the same techniques as with air import cargo. In 1985, some 3,679,779 pieces of containerized cargo were processed in Hong Kong.

There is regular scheduled ferry service between Hong Kong and the Chinese mainland. This daily service is very popular and over 625,000 passengers a year use this service whose terminal is at Tai Kok Tsui, Kowloon, in the colony.

Passengers arriving from Macao do so by scheduled ferries, jetfoils and hydrofoils at the Hong Kong & Kowloon -Macao Ferry Terminal. Almost 8,000,000 passengers a year use this service.

The service also has the aptly-named Strike and Search Division to patrol its convoluted coastline and its internal waters and over 230 islands. The service uses a fleet of launches and inflatable craft in its strike and search operations around the colony.

There are other border crossing areas between the colony and mainland China and these are being increased to handle the greater traffic between the two.

In addition to the two checkpoints, one at Lo Wu and the other at Man Kam To, for rail and road traffic respectively on the Chinese-British colony border, a new entry point for passenger traffic with hover-ferries plying between Shatin and Meisha, China, started operations in August, 1984. Almost 20,000 passengers from China arrive daily by ordinary train at Lo Wu. There are almost 2,000 additional daily passengers on a special non-stop train coming from Guangzhou and arriving at the Hung Hom railway station in Kowloon. Another 240 daily passengers arriving on coaches are processed at Man Kam To. So far, the new hover-ferry between Shatin and Meisha carries an average of about 35 passengers daily. However, the goods imported from China and processed at the Man Kam To checkpoint by motor vehicle was over 1,135,000 tons in 1985.

Officers of the Customs Investigation Bureau operate in plain clothes. They investigate offenses in connection with narcotics, copyright infringement, and other illegal activities. They also coordinate information and intelligence related to smuggling and drug trafficking. Last year they arrested almost 1,500 persons in connection with narcotics offenses and seized over 600 pounds of narcotics.

The Copyright Division investigates infringement on musical, artistic and literary works, sound recordings, films, cassettes and discs. The Intelligence and Investigation Division maintains critical records, keeps track of suspected persons, details of crews, and cargo importers.

The Trade Controls Operations Branch conducts factory and consignment inspections in support of the Certificate of Origin system. For certain goods imported into the United States which may affect international agreements entered into by the United States, a product must be accompanied by a certificate of origin. If you import such articles, you would want your supplier to conform with the U.S. regulations and obtain an appropriate Certificate of Origin for each shipment destined to you.

The Trade Controls Operations Branch is the organization you would appeal to if you had a complaint. They will investigate. They will mediate, if appropriate. In 1985, they investigated and handled 813 trade complaints and conducted 54,371 inspections of factories, consignment, and reserved commodity declarations.

Another group with almost the same name, the Trade Controls Investigation Branch of the Customs and Excise Service deals with counterfeiting, trade mark forgeries, false trade descriptions, and industrial copyright infringement. It also is the leading edge in investigating compliance with textile quotas, something very dear to the United States textile and garment industry. There are good textile and clothing possibilities in Hong Kong which is the explanation behind these quotas and the need for Hong Kong to police this aspect of their export trade.

Bear in mind that business is similar in most countries. If you have a patent on a product that you would like to see manufactured in Hong Kong, there is an office there to register your intellectual or real property. Then always mention this to any potential manufacturer to prevent any temptation to pirate your design.

DEPENDENCE ON EXPORTS

A good understanding of your supplier's industry and country will always help you focus on the right type of product to search for. This is part of the study phase outlined earlier. The more you learn about a country or a political entity like Hong Kong, the clearer the import possibilities will be for you.

Owing to its heavy dependence on exports, Hong Kong's manufacturing industry continued to benefit in 1984 and 1985 from the economic recovery in most of its trading markets, in particular the United States. Between 1983 and 1984, exports rose 32 percent.

The major factors that have given Hong Kong its international reputation as a leading manufacturing and commercial center continued to work well. Low taxes on earnings and profits, free enterprise and trade, an energetic workforce and good port facilities all contribute to Hong Kong's growth. It has maintained consistent commercial policies and excellent worldwide communications.

The manufacturing sector is the mainstay of the colony's economy. It accounts for 22 percent of the gross domestic product and 38 percent of the total employment. Experts claim that up to 90% of the colony's production is eventually exported. Light manufacturing industries, producing mainly consumer products, predominate.

About 68 per cent of the total industrial work force is employed in the textiles, clothing, electronics, plastic products, toys, watches, and clocks industry. These industries all together accounted for three-quarters of the colony's total exports in 1985, a pattern which experts predict will continue.

Many new and more advanced techniques are being used to improve products offered for sale, much of this improvement has been attributed to the competition from other countries with low labor costs. In the case of textiles and clothing, many of the improvements have resulted from pressure at the other end of the marketplace: the demand for better, upscale products and the various protectionism adopted in some of the main export markets of Hong Kong.

In order to be competitive in areas needing a high level of technology where the manufacturers needed newer buildings than the usual two-story factory buildings common in Hong Kong, the government set aside about 100 acres of land for a modern industrial park called the Tai Po Industrial Estate. A second larger one, of over 150 acres, is planned at Yuen Long. Almost 100 applications to locate in the new parks have been approved.

The government also has constructed four-story industrial buildings ready-to-move-into for lease to companies ready-to-go. In eight other sites, the government has placed over 500,000 suare feet into industry in 1985 alone.

Hong Kong has started to send industrial investment promotion missions to the industrialized nations like the United

States, Japan, Australia, France, West Germany, Italy and Australia to meet potential partners and to visit industries with the latest developments. Special attention is given to any industry expressing an interest in locating in Hong Kong. The United States remains the largest source of overseas industrial investment in Hong Kong with 54% of the total. Japan is in second place with 21%, and Britain is a distant third with 7%.

The textile and clothing industries are the largest. Together they employ 41% of the total industrial workforce and produce 40% of the total value of domestic exports. The output of cotton yarn in 1984 was over 330 million pounds, a huge production, but it had declined since the year before.

Production of man-made fiber blended yarn was 44 million pounds and the production of woolen and worsted yard was almost nine million pounds. In the weaving trade, there are almost 20,000 looms operating and producing almost 800,000,000 million square yards of woven fabrics, of which 92% was cotton. Interestingly, almost all the cotton goods were exported as is but the virtual totality of the other upgrade woven goods was absorbed by the local garment manufacturers to produce finished clothing, mostly for export.

More than 50 million pounds of knitted fabrics were exported, 72% of which was cotton and the remainder was of man-made fibers.

Hong Kong also performs considerable finishing like bleaching, dyeing, printing and finishing. These processes include texturising, multi-color roller and screen printing, pre-shrinking, permanent pressing and polymerising.

The range of products produced by the light industrial group, particularly electronics and plastics, has been described earlier. The watch industry produces both mechanical and electronic watches as well as subassemblies like cases, watch bands, movements and dials. An importer should remember that subassemblies are sometimes duty-free while the finished product has a high duty. This explains why some companies concentrate on the final assembly of parts imported from overseas.

In terms of dollar volume some products have proven to be quite popular and this is reflected in the export volume recorded by the authorities in Hong Kong:

Clothing	Plastic Toys and Dolls
Jewellry	Goldwares and Silverwares
Artificial Flowers	Household Appliances
Transister Apparatus	Recording Equipment
Photographic Equipment	Optical Goods
Watches and Clocks	Office Machines
Data Processing Equipment	Textiles
Perfume materials	Plumbing and Lighting
Footwear	Handbags

There are many other articles, such as road vehicles, even air-cushioned vehicles, and other heavy machinery and machine tools that are produced in Hong Kong.

Some products are difficult to handle, either they are controlled closely in Hong Kong; an example being carved ivory or general ivoryware as a part of protection of endangered species, or the protection can be at the U.S. end for the same reason.

Trade Marks, Patents, Copyrights and other forms of proprietory interest can be protected in Hong Kong, but the forms of protection require action in Hong Kong whether or not they may be protected because of registration in the United Kingdom.

Anyone desiring to register a Trade Mark can get a free application form from the Trade Marks Registry in the Registrar General's Department. However, patents in Hong Kong are granted when these patents have been approved and accepted as a United Kingdom patent or a European Patent in the U.K. The important thing to remember is that original grants of patent are non-existent in Hong Kong so registration and acceptance must take place in a country granting patents and then the registration has to have an approved trail of acceptances through Europe to Hong Kong.

The Registrar General's office also records the names of companies incorporated or licensed to do business in the colony. Formally, all companies incorporated in Hong Kong or all foreign companies that have established a place of business in the colony are recorded in the department.

There had been a filing or registration fee of about US$50. for a Hong Kong incorporation plus an amount less than US$1.00 per every US$125 of nominal capital. Registration fees for foreign companies establishing an office in Hong Kong is somewhat less expensive.

LABOR FACTORS

Hong Kong has no mandatory or minimum wage standard. Wages are affected by the basic forces of supply and demand. They are determined similarly as in North America; that is, by the daily, hourly, weekly, monthly, or piece work basis. Manufacturing labor is generally paid every two weeks, and most other wage-earners are paid monthly. The overall average daily labor wage is about US$ 12.00. In addition to normal benefits like paid holidays and paid leave, many receive subsidized meals or food allowances, bonuses for regular attendance, medical benefits, and the 13th month annual bonus. Some employers provide lodging and transportation.

Normally women are not permitted to work between 8 p.m. and 6 a.m., but certain exceptions have been granted in the cotton-spinning industry.

Workmen's compensation for on-the-job-injuries for the worker or the worker's family is new and compulsory. Labor Inspectors have been pressing for convictions of employers who work children and illegal aliens.

The trade unions have an apparent ideological affiliation. In early 1985 there were 383 employees' unions with about 352,000 members plus a few other types of unions, some with both employers and employees. Only about one-third of the union members are independent of apparent political affiliation or ideological affiliation. There are 73 unions that are considered "friendly" toward the People's Republic of China, mainland China, and are affiliated under the umbrella of the Hong Kong Federation of Trade Unions.

Work stoppages are not very serious and the total number of workdays lost are minimal by North American standards. Most grievances are individual claims for wages in light of adequate notice, severance pay, arrears and compensatory wages in lieu of time off. The local "labour" department employees investigate complaints and provide arbitration when possible. The department also maintains employment offices to assist those seeking jobs.

HONG KONG'S RELATIONSHIPS

About half of all Hong Kong's imports are purchased from China and Japan together. The United States is a distant third. Yet, the United States is in first place, buying almost 45% of everything Hong Kong produces for foreign buyers. The United States alone buys twice as much from Hong Kong as the next three countries combined: China, United Kingdom and West Germany.

The colony's statisticians keep tabs on the Consumer Price Index according to about 50% of the urban households that spend between US$ 128 and US$ 449.00 per month and another C.P.I. for 30% of the urban households that spend between US$ 450.00 and US$834.00 per month. The benchmark year is that ending in September 1980. Both groups increased about 57 points in four years.

A third C.P.I. is called the Hang Seng Consumer Price Index which also uses the same base year and covers the 10% of the urban Household group spending between US$ 835.00 and US$ 2,565.00 per month. This one rose by 60 points in four years. In the same time period the United States C.P.I. rose by 64 points.

Several countries have a dominate position in Hong Kong's relationships. The United Kingdom has ruled it for over a century and has a decade to go. The colony will revert to China which shares a common language and is its biggest and most important trading partner, except for the United States. When combined imports and exports are considered together, the United States is the leading trading partner, followed by China and then Japan.

Anyone who entertains the desire to take advantage of the numerous well-priced products available from Hong Kong for mail order enterprises in North America will want to establish good relationships in the colony. Time should be spent to cultivate good relationships in China because in a few years the colony and the mainland will be getting closer and the North American importer familiar with both markets will be in the best position to further his business opportunities.

Mainland China does not directly compete with Hong Kong's suppliers except for the colony's re-exported goods. Traders in Hong Kong are quick to leap onto any Chinese-made product that seems to attract buyers abroad. If you have an exclusive idea for a product that may be well-priced and available in China, it would be best to explore your chances to get it directly before revealing your ideas to a supplier in Hong Kong who could take your idea and sell it to the world in the wink of an eye.

On July 11, 1997 the People's Republic of China will establish the new Hong Kong. It will enjoy a high degree of autonomy except in foreign and military affairs.

The Chinese have promised that the laws currently in force in Hong Kong will remain basically unchanged. Individuals holding administrative and police jobs may be kept on. Regardless of the lengthy declaration between China and the United Kingdom to describe the agreement of the switchover between the British and the Chinese, it is obvious that there will be changes and it will be wise to learn how to deal with each as soon as possible.

Both countries have agreed to establish working groups and councils to jointly agree on administrative actions which, although taken now, will affect the colony's affairs well after July 1, 1997. For example, a committee on land leases has been established and extends into the division of rents earned as they arise from leases executed after the date of their declaration: 19 December 1984.

The basic lifestyle of the colony is meant to remain unchanged until the year 2047, fifty years from the takeover.

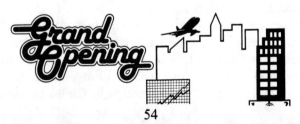

Chapter Three

FINDING A PRODUCT IN CHINA "The Last Frontier."

Note! This is not step three. *But I thought I would provide you with some important information about China, the world's last frontier for low, low, wholesale prices.*

China's new goal in Foreign Trade relies heavily on exploiting every aspect of economic relations to foster its internal development.

At the highest level of government is the Ministry of Foreign Trade. A series of state-controlled trading units called corporations have been established for major product lines, for both export and import. These are political organizations with functional business responsibilities. They cannot be circumvented as trade in communist countries is rigidly controlled. It can be slow-moving but once your idea has been accepted, doors will fly open.

Virtually all regulations and procedures to operate and expand a sector of the business economy has been submitted for and received approval by the State Council. When you suggest a change to an established policy, it may take over a year to get approval - and that is when they agree with you! Try to work with the system. The key element is that the Chinese want to make deals.

They are willing to barter, pay, and joint venture. They admit this is a period of "readjustment" and that they will favor anything that helps their exports and self-financing. An example of barter trading has occurred with a Japanese customer whereby China exported coal and received machinery, equipment, and foodstuffs. China is particularly open to acquiring machinery to process exactly what you want, China will supply all the labor, and earn a fee which is applied against the value of the machinery. After China has earned the full value of the machinery, your equity in the machinery is down to zero and you will start paying a higher pre-established fee for the manufacturing process.

The Chinese Export Commodities Fair is held in Guangzhou, formerly Canton, twice a year. Only Chinese products are displayed, primarily for export. Attendance is by invitation and you must apply through one of the official "corporations" or from an official China government agent or agency, such as the china Resources Company. The Canton Trade Fair, its former identity, is famous. From Hong Kong, the city is three hours by express train; by plane it is 30 minutes.

All guests are met by an English-speaking or French-speaking, whatever you are, representative who will escort you and your party to your hotel.

China. Mainland China. The sleeping giant. Red China. The People's republic of China. The Great Wall of China. This conjures up all the fantasies of a mystery, the mysterious Orient. The closed doors. The barriers. All this is now changing. It has taken forty years for the doors to open.

While it is only a little larger in size than the United States, it has five times more people, over one billion! Over 94% are Han Chinese, with the remaining ethnic groups mostly Mongol, Korean, Manchu and others. The official language is Mandarin Chinese. There are a number of important dialects, particularly associated with large cities dominating certain regions, like Shanghai and Canton.

Shanghai, historically one of the world's great ports that gave its name to the English language when drunks were rolled in San Francisco and *shanghaied* in the service of sailing ships. It is a communist country that has been at odds with the Soviet Union for almost a generation. Paradoxically, it has been courting favor with the United States commercially and culturally for over a decade.

During this period it has opened up business opportunities wherever it has been able and has been structuring facilities, like new hotels for business and tourists, and trade organizations to help foreigners, especially westerners of whom the

56

Americans are at the forefront. Their currency unit is a Yuan. The official rate had stayed level, more or less, at around 3 Yuan for 1 U.S. dollar.

Several trade organizations have been established for importers in North America to find suppliers and producers of mail order-type of articles and products. These are official Chinese government agencies and as such will be best able to cut through the maze of language, currency exchanges, and acutely different business customs. For example, there is no corporate law in China. There really is no business law or commercial law as westerners would expect. Arbitration clauses in contracts are virtually useless although the Chinese are starting to recognize that they will have to adopt some method of arbitration acceptable to businessmen in other countries.

There are 19 radios per 100 Chinese and only 1½ television sets per 100 Chinese. The circulation of newspapers is only 7 per 100 people, and there are only 2 telephones per 100 people. Bear in mind, this includes business and governmental telephones, too.

Names and the spelling of important names have changed and a new map may be a worthwhile investment. The capital, Peking, is now Beijing. The westernized city of Canton is now Guangzhou. Spellings are vary between the so-called official Chinese *pinyin* version and the traditional anglicized version. Remember the dictum of "while in Rome...". It is better to accept the Chinese version. However, Chunking can also be spelled Tchong-King or Chongqing, depending on one's reference book. If you pronounce these phonetically, you will see or note that they mean the same thing.

If you are planning a business trip into China, more than usual advance preparations are definitely in order to make it pleasing personally and worthwhile businesswise. Ask your contacts to have English-speaking personnel available to meet you upon arrival at the airport. You will want to have accommodations at a level of quality you have learned to expect in the United States. If you are a seasoned traveller off-the-beaten-path, nothing will bother you.

For the individual who has not travelled a great deal, China will be a real adventure. Businessmen who have travelled to China in the last few years have reported a number of hotels or accommodations are reasonably good and a few new hotels are just about ready for business and should be good. Nothing is guaranteed, but the following are supposed to be as good as you can get in China:

Guangzhou (formerly Canton)	The Garden Hotel
Nanjing	Jinling Hotel
Wuhan	Qingchuan Hotel
Beijing (formerly Peking)	Jianguo Hotel Beijing-Toronto Hotel Holiday Inn Lido Hotel Great Wall Sheraton Hotel State Guest Houses Zhaolung Hotel Kun Lun Hotel
Chongking	Renmin Hotel
Hangzhou	Hangzhou (formerly Xiling) Hotel
Guilin	Li River Hotel (sometimes written Lijiang) State Guest House Banyan Lake Hotel #5
Shanghai	Jinjiang Hotel Cypress Hotel Shanghai Mansion Shanghai Hotel

58

The People's Republic of China is such a huge country that there may be many cities you may be interested in. You should consult a competent travel agent well in advance of your trip.

It is almost impossible to go anywhere in China without permission or approbation in advance. The businessman has the best opportunity to be escorted to wherever the products he wants are produced. The China Resources Company, the official agent in Hong Kong, is an example of the key ally to have on your side.

The People's Bank of China is the central bank of the country. There is a branch in New York. It has correspondent arrangements with 960 banks in 144 countries. It can issue banking credit and help you acquire favorable terms.

There are a few branches in Paris, Tokyo, London and Sidney, and has five main branches in China: Beijing, Shanghai, Tianjin, Guangzhou and Fujian.

In China itself, the administrative office in charge of exchange control is the State General Administration of Exchange Control which must O.K. any payment-in-kind or any value-in-kind for, say, a situation where you provided parts and subassemblies, and the final assembly and testing would take place by Chinese. Another example is where the entire manufacturing is taking place in China, but perhaps at four or five different locations or cities.

As eager as the Chinese are to establish worthwhile joint ventures and are eager for foreign capital or capital goods, it is unlikely that they would want a minority position. Since there is no corporate law in China, all the provisions and terms must be spelled out in considerable detail in the original articles of association. The Chinese will put up land, factory, labor, raw materials and most reluctantly, any cash.

Once you have decided to seriously explore the possibility of acquiring products in China, you will need some help to determine which of the official corporations is the one to send your inquiry to.

As indicated earlier in the previous chapter, the Economic Section of the Chinese Embassy in Washington should be able to help you acquire the precise first address you will need.

There are a few organizations in Beijing the capital, that specialize in finding the right address for you. One is the "China International Trust and Investment Corporation" and the other is the "China Council for the Promotion of International Trade." The CCPIT specializes in bringing buyer and seller together. It also handles all Trademark registrations, patents, copyrights, and disputes. Both of these can be addressed in Beijing.

Some of the trading corporations whose main export interests have been made known are listed here:

China National Light Industrial
Products Import and Export Corporation
82 Donganmen Street
Beijing, P.R.O. CHINA

Sewing machines and spare parts; bicycles and spare parts; enamelware, aluminumware; thermos bottles; rubber shoes; leather products; suitcases; locks, clocks and watches; toilet soaps; detergents; zip fasteners; kerosene cooking stoves; paper; pencils; flashlights and batteries; electric fans; fluorescent tubes; stationery; sports goods; alarm clocks; musical instruments; flooring tiles; decorative lamps; plywood; and leather shoes.

China Silk Corporation
82 Donganmen Street
Beijing, P.R.O. CHINA

White steam filature; tussah silk yarn; spun silk yarn; silk tops; silk noils; pure silk piece goods; spun silk pongee; nail poplin; embroidered dresses, garments, scarfs and neckties; rayon goods; - and their Shanghai office specializes in silk shirts for men; pyjamas; women's blouses and skirts; scarfs and other silk or rayon items.

China National Arts and Crafts Import
and Export Corporaiton
82 Donganmen Street
Beijing, P.R.O. CHINA

Pottery and porcelain; embroidery and drawnwork; diamonds; cultured pearls; jewellry; ivory and jade carvings; mahogany furniture; lacquered wooden furniture; curios; embroidered shoes; woven bamboo, straw or wicker basketry; reed shades; tubular steel; wood furniture and artificial flowers. Quilt cover sets and bedspreads; aprons and guest towels; pillowcases and breakfast sets; fur animals; wooden toys; slippers and casual shoes; wood louver windows; kites; horn chess pieces; painting scrool knobs; artistic pictures of shell and feathers; Songhua inkslabs; artistic candles; chopsticks; wooden frames.

China National Textiles Import
and Export Corporation
82 Donganmen Street
Beijing, P.R.O. CHINA

Cotton, raw wool; yarns and threads; grey, bleached and dyed; yarn-dyed piece goods; blended fabrics; worsted and woolen piece goods; plush; camelwool; garments for men, women and children; infants' sets; cotton manufactured goods; woolen blankets; prints, sweaters and trousers; cashmere sweaters; petticoats, briefs, socks, face towels; bedsheets and pillowcases; terry; T-shirts and vests; pyjamas, frocks and nightgowns; Trueran-cotton fabrics.

China National Native Produce and Animal
By-Products Import and Export Corporation
82 Donganmen Street
Beijing, P.R.O. CHINA

Rosin, raw lacquer; black tea; green tea; jute, gunny sacks, polysacks; fireworks and firecrackers; candles; black fungus; apricot kernels; synthetic camphor; dried chillies and honey; walnuts and peach kernels; peppermint oils; menthol crystals; fluecured tobacco leaf; rugs and carpets; turpentine; citric acid; paulownia logs; fur and leather garments; dried fruits and medicinal herbs; medicated liquor; scarves; closed-back and open-backed carpets; Han court carpets; artistic draperies and blossom carpets; hooked rugs; silk carpets; dehydrated vegetables; dried fruits; pen-brushes.

All of these corporations have branch offices and provincial offices which may specialize in particular products or product lines and the corporation may refer you there. The Chinese recommend that you reproduce several copies of your proposal or your inquiry and to send them to different addresses, as well as to some of the trade service organizations like CCPIT and CITIC.

North American investors who wish to start joint ventures in China may get in touch directly with appropriate Chinese corporations or other economic organizations and consultancy groups. If these cannot help find the suitable partner in China, an investor can then write directly to the Ministry of Foreign Economic Relations and Trade, the CITIC or to a development corporation of a specific province, autonomous region, or municipality, giving them all the particulars and asking them for recommendations for appropriate suppliers or partners.

The Chinese organization is not built for speed and the North American importer should be patient as he develops alternate sources of products. The importer may get a bit impatient and try to telephone. Even if the Chinese counterpart has a telephone, it is very difficult for most Chinese to handle English on the phone, just as it will be for most reading this book to try to handle Chinese on the telephone.

Generally, the Chinese will correspond in English, letting the translators prepare the letters. Often, however, the translators know English reasonably well but do not know the technical word-of-the-art.

The more you know your subject, the more important does it become for you to have your draft-letter reviewed by someone who is not an expert. Ask the person to read it and to comment on it. Tell the person in advance you want a tough review, a critical review of your message, not necessarily the business side of it, just the clarity of the English. If you do not have unmanageable pride, you will learn a great deal. If the reviewer cannot handle it in the good old mother tongue, how is the fellow in China supposed to understand?

The example is a bit like the tourist in a foreign country who insists on talking English to an eight-year-old who never heard any language than his own. As the tourist starts to realize he is not understood, he starts to emphasize his words by shouting. Instead of making things easier, he has made them irretrievably worse.

In writing a good business letter of introduction of yourself, your idea, the product you hope to find, and all the elements that are important to you, you should carefully prepare your outline. Introduce one technical thought at a time. Discipline yourself to define the thought in at least two different ways, — by putting yourself in your reader's shoes, you will help him understand the first time. He will recognize your efforts and in return he will do the same even if he has to box the translator's ears.

The Chinese will invite you to visit China to meet the right people. Until you are very comfortable with the replies you have received and your instincts tell you the making of the right deal is at hand, do not rush into the premature expense of a trip until everything that can be worked out by correspondence has been done.

Eventually everything must be reduced to writing. Keep copies of all your correspondence and of all incoming replies. Remember that there is no corporate law, and virtually no business and commercial law as you know it. The Chinese do not like third-party arbitration, they prefer negotiation.. for thousands of centuries, China has negotiated...time is on the side of the sleeping giant. In other words, you may end up discounting your potential loss through arbitration because China has staying power.

A few other Chinese corporations that may be of interest are:

China National Foreign Trade Transportation Corp.
Er Li Gou, Xi Jian
Beijing, P. R. O. CHINA

China National Metals and Minerals
  Import and Export Corp.
Er Li Gou
Beijing, P. R. O. CHINA

China Buildings Materials Export Supply Corporation
Bai Wan Zhuang
Beijing, P. R. O. CHINA

China Automotive Industry Corporation
12 Fuxingmenwai St.
Beijing, P. R. O. CHINA

China North Industries Corporation
7A Yuetab Bab Jie
P. O. Box 2137
Beijing, P. R. O. CHINA

China Great Wall Industrial Corporation
17 Xidang Wenchang Hutong
P. O. Box 847
Beijing, People's Republic of CHINA

China National Machinery Import and Export Corp.
Er Ligou, Xijiao
P. O. Box 49
Beijing, P. R. O. CHINA

Oriental Scientific Instruments Import and Export Corp.
52 Sanlihe Road, Western District
Beijing, P. R. O. CHINA

China Electronics Import and Export Corp.
49 Fuxing Road
P. O. Box 140
Beijing, P. R. O. CHINA

China National Instrument Import and Export Corp.
Erligoum Xijiao
P. O. Box 2811
Beijing, P. R. O. CHINA

Chapter Four

MADE IN TAIWAN

The Taiwanese are among the most aggressive and successful exporters in the world. It is virtually impossible to browse through a large retail outlet in the United States without seeing goods "Made in Taiwan" being carried to the check-out counters.

Only the size of Maryland and Delaware combined, Taiwan has a population of over 19,000,000 most of whom are Han Chinese but only 18% are from the mainland, the remainder being native of Formosa. In 1949, the Kumintang government of Generalissimo Chiang Kai-shek fled the mainland with almost 2,000,000 supporters as the communists took over the mainland. Taiwan is a sore subject with the mainland Chinese and has been for almost forty years since 1949.

Despite the loss of diplomatic status with the United States on December 15, 1978, the Taiwanese have maintained a steady growth in their exports to North America. They maintain a Coordination Council for North American Affairs in Washington, D.C. and elsewhere instead of an embassy. The United States maintains an "American Institute" in the capital city of Taipei instead of an embassy. The loss of diplomatic recognition was the price the United States paid to open diplomatic doors with the mainland People's Republic of China.

In recent years, Taiwan's products have been transformed from those with a labor-intensive basis to one based on high technology as well as on a capital-intensive heavy industrial base.

The industrial sector does more than turn out light industrial products like footwear, textiles, sporting goods and processed food, but also heavy industrial products such as machinery, transportation equipment, electrical and electronic products, computers and computer peripherals.

In addition to the Coordination Council for North American Affairs (CCNAA), the Taiwanese maintain offices

65

of the China External Trade Development Council (CETDC) and the Far East Trade Service, Inc. (FETS). These will help you for trade purposes with Taiwan suppliers.

The China External Trade Development Council and the Far East Trade Service, Inc. are interchangeable in that they are part and parcel of the same non-profit organization funded by both the government of Taiwan and various Taiwanese business associations.

The CETDC was founded first in 1970 with headquarters in Taipei. Its sister organization was established a year later, 1971, and offers professional services to foreign businessmen to help them conduct their business in Taiwan.

While many of the activities of these two organizations overlap, CETDC appears to be more of the chamber of commerce-type. It maintains a Trade Mart at the Taipei Sungshan International Airport. This is an important shopping center for visiting importers. There are about 150 shops each with a showroom and manned by qualified salespeople.

CETDC also sponsors design and packaging seminars to train Taiwanese industrial designers in an effort to be responsive to the world market. It has even established a special laboratory to help Taiwanese manufacturers improve their selection of materials for packaging and their actual packaging techniques.

CETDC established the Taipei World Trade Center (TWTC) in 1980 to promote foreign trade. In the organization's Exhibition Complex are held local and international trade shows. Underway is a new headquarters to house the trade mart, offices and a deluxe commercial hotel. Virtually every type of commercial office will be housed in the new building: trade promotion organizations, trade offices, consulates, customs, postal and telecommunications, banks, brokers and forwarders, shipping agents, travel agencies, insurance agents and government offices.

Together, the CETDC and the FETS will process and reply to all trade inquiries from North American businesspersons. They will provide lists of Taiwan suppliers as well as trade and product information. They will arrange meetings with government officials, local manufacturers and exporters.

To keep foreign businessmen in tune with the latest economic developments and sources of products, they publish *Trade Opportunities in Taiwan,* an English-language weekly which contains import inquiries and export offers as well as significant industrial and business news. It lists trade promotion activities and monthly trade statistics. Other publications you can ask for are:

Taiwan Products

An illustrated monthly magazine published in English, Japanese, French, Spanish, German and Arabic. A single product line is featured each month.

Exports of the Republic of China

These periodically-updated publications contain major export commodities and the names of the leading exporters.

There are also market surveys and reports on trade regulations which will be helpful for the North American importer who knows which product line he will be dealing in. The publications are generated by groupings of suppliers or exporters of a common product line of Taiwanese goods.

The CETDC/FETS often organizes participation by Taiwanese exporters in trade shows in North America and elsewhere. It occasionally will sponsor a "solo show" in which only products made in Taiwan are featured. They participate in over 100 established trade shows around the world each year.

Reverse shows are also sponsored. There have been two recent European Trade Exhibitions in Taipei.

There is a permanent export products display with over 1,700 booths at the Export Mart on the second and third floors of the terminal building at Taipei's Sungshan International Airport and is open during normal business hours during the week and in the forenoon on Saturdays.

Once a local office of CETDC/FETS is aware of your interests it will inform you every time a Taiwanese exporter of goods you are interested in is going to be in your region. They will permit you to meet with the representative while he is in your region.

It is best to start by corresponding with or telephoning the appropriate trade office closest to you:

FETRACO, Inc.
P. O. Box 349
Place Bonaventure
Montreal, Quebec H5A 1B5   Tel: (514) 866 0598

Far East Trade Service, Inc.
2 Bloor Street East
Toronto, Ontario M4W 1A8   Tel: (416) 922- 2412

Far East Trade Service, Inc.
409 Granville Street
Vancouver, British Columbia V6C 1T2   Tel: (604) 682 9501

Economic Division, CCNAA
4301 Connecticut Avenue, N.W.
Suite 420
Washington, D.C. 20008   Tel: (202) 686 9501

Investment and Trade Office, CCNAA
8th Floor
126 East 56th Street
New York, NY 10022   Tel: (212) 752 2340

CETDC, Inc.
41 Madison Avenue
New York, NY 10010   Tel: (212) 532 7055

Commercial Division, CCNAA
19th Floor
20 North Clark Street
Chicago, Illinois 60602   Tel: (312) 332 2535

Far East Trade Service, Inc.
The Merchantile Mart   Suite 272
Chicago, Illinois 60654   Tel: (312) 321 9338

Commercial Division, CCNAA
Suite 2150
1360 Post Oak Boulevard
Houston, Texas 77056   Tel: (713) 961 9794

Commercial Division, CCNAA
3660 Wilshire Boulevard
Suite 918
Los Angeles, California 90010   Tel: (213) 380 3644
FETS Representative
555 Montgomery Street
San Francisco, California 94111   Tel: (415) 362 6882

To better appreciate how much volume is sent to the United States annually by Taiwan, consider that Taiwan ships over US$ 12 billion to the U.S.A., as compared to about US$ 10 billion from Hong Kong to the U.S.A.

Taiwan is particularly happy with the success of its industrial products on the world market. It has become even more aggressive since it lost diplomatic status with its chief market and ally, the United States.

In the first stages of Taiwan's economic development after 1949, industrial products accounted for only 8.1% of its total exports. The high rate of sustained economic and industrial growth in the following years resulted in industrial products making up 81% of total exports in 1971.

By 1979 the ratio was boosted even higher, with industrial products totalling 90.5% that year, and in 1983 it reached 93.1%. Taiwan has been moving constantly toward industrialization. Its products have taken on a greater percentage of the market around the world and even the range of product-types has expanded. In particular, the quality of its products has improved and making them more competitive worldwide.

Agricultural products and processed agricultural goods made a significant contribution in the early years and has grown but not as dramatically as industrial products. Overall, the dollars amounts of exports has risen, but the proportion has fallen from 22.1% to just under 7% of the total export trade.

Taiwan started exporting sugar, rice and bananas. Later, processed products like canned pineapple, canned mushrooms, canned asparagus and other items gained entry into the world market.

In order of importance the make-up of exported products is dominated by electronics:

Commodity Groups "Made in Taiwan"	Percentage Share of Total Exports
Electronics	15.0%
Textile Garments	10.8
Fibers, Yarns, Fabrics	6.2
Footwear	7.7
Toys, Sporting Goods Hunting/Fishing Goods	6.0
Wood Products/Furniture	4.9
Metal Products	5.4
Machinery	3.8
Transportation Equipment	4.1
Plastic Products	3.4
Household electric applicances	2.2
Electrical Machinery	2.1
Iron and Steel	2.5
Refined Petroleum Products	1.8
Other textile goods	1.4
Canned and Preserved Foods	1.1
Pottery, Earthenware	1.1
Watches and Clocks	0.8
Photo/Optical Goods	1.0
Rubber products	0.8
Fishery Products	1.1
Miscellaneous others	16.3
	100.0%

Electronic products rank first in Taiwan's export commodities. In 1983 their total export value was US$ 3.8 billion and accounted for 15% of the total exports of US$ 25.1 billion, to all countries around the world. This grand total was 24.5% over the previous year's total!

In that same year, the value of exports of electronic products taken together with that of electrical machinery and apparatus and of household electrical products amounted to US$ 4.9 billion, or 19.3% of total exports.

Taiwan's remarkable growth has continued. The official records show that in the first half of 1985, electronic products earned export income of US$ 2.4 billion, up 49.4% over the corresponding period a year earlier. The major overseas markets for these products are the United States, Hong Kong, West Germany, and Britain. It is important to point out that virtually 99% of all electronics exported to Hong Kong are re-exported by Hong Kong to other overseas markets.

Garments made from textile fabrics rank second in Taiwan's export commodities. In 1985, total export value was US$ 2.7 billion amounting to 10.8% of the total exports and representing a modest 2.4% growth over the preceding year's volume. The major markets for this group of commodities are the United States, Saudi Arabia, Japan, West Germany and Canada.

When ordering from an experienced exporter like Taiwan, most suppliers will offer price lists in U.S. dollars. Prices may be quoted in several currencies including the New Taiwan dollar. The approximate exchange rate has been: one T$1.00 = two and a half US cents; or 40 T$ = 1US$, the latter meaning forty Taiwan dollars are equal to one United States dollar.

Taiwan has some of the best export statistics and information retrieval systems to help a North American importer focus on a special range of products or a well defined product line, as well as for semi-manufactured assemblies for final assembly in the importer country.

Of the three supplier-source markets discussed in this chapter, the Taiwanese will probably set the standard by which other countries, other than Japan, in the orient will be measured. Japan's manufacturing and industrial base is so overwhelming in the world that Japan is in a class by itself.

Consequently, the North American importer should carefully define the type of products the importer is seeking, or the importer should ask the corresponding Taiwan agency or field office to provide a detailed definition of the range of products falling into a commodity heading.

Ask plenty of questions. Answers may differ. For example, one Taiwanese definition of "Electrical Machinery and Apparatus" is:

Data processing systems
Consumer Electronics
Electronic parts, components and accessories
Electrical home appliances
Communication equipment
Heavy electric equipment
Illuminating equipment
Batteries
Measuring and Test equipment
Electrical wires and cables

However, in a listing by internationally accepted commodity listings, the Taiwanese category recorded as "Electrical Machineries and Apparatus" contains the following subheadings:
Radio cassette
Telephone sets
Electric fans for domestic use
Linear integrated circuits
NTSC system color TV broadcast receivers
   (USA/Canada-type)
Parts of computer
Radio broadcast receiver incorporating
   record player and audio tape
   recorder and player
Cordless telephone system
Frequency converter
RETMA black and white TV receivers
Parts of television apparatus
Rocket electronic calculator
Terminal
Digital IC
TV Channel Selectors
Peripheral
Electrical apparatus similar to switches, relays and the like

Micro motor
Cassette deck and recorder
LED tube display
Germanium diodes
Color closed circuit TV
Middle range speaker
Lamps and lighting fittings of base metal
Radio receiver
Parts and apparatus for TV receivers, FM-AM receiver
    and the like
Parts of electrical apparatus for making connections to
    or in electrical circuits
Speaker system with enclosure
Rectifiers
Ceramic capacitors of low voltage under 50 MFD
Carbon film resistors, fixed
Cathode ray tubes for color television receivers
Parts of micro-computer
Electrical switch

The North American importer is well advised to probe for details since one definition may not be as precise or as informative as another. The buyer can often get ideas that are not always where they might seem. If the Taiwanese are proud to publicize that US$ 38 million of frozen shrimp is exported to the U.S.A., this could hint that this product is well established and would NOT be a promising new line for an importer to start a mail order business with.

A broad-brush look at products sold mostly to other countries can help to illustrate the importance of picking up data and taking the time to study it. Japan and Saudi Arabia import most of Taiwan's fresh and chilled bananas. Japan buys more duck feathers, twenty times more than the next four countries combined. Japan and Belgium buy most of the duck down. Most of the Rice japonica (ponlai), polished, is sold, you would guess, to Japan — but, no — It is sold to Indonesia and Madagascar.

Almost the entire production of canned white asparagus is shipped to West Germany and France. Textured yarn of continuous polyester fibers is sold to Pakistan, Japan, Hong Kong and Singapore; and woven fabric of pure continuous synthetic textile materials goes to Hong Kong, Singapore and Saudi Arabia. Yet the biggest buyer of spun yarn of 50 to 84% discontinuous polyester fibers is purchased by Australia. Nigeria imports most of the Strand yard of synthetic fiber mixed with regenerated fiber.

Virturally every type of wearing apparel for men, women or children is sold primarily to the United States market, except for fabric sport shoes and boots. The United States imports over US$ 132,000,000 of bicycles from Taiwan yearly and US$ 18 million in bicycle parts. In some categories like sun glasses and cameras, the entire production line is produced primarily for the United States. This is also true for quartz watches, TV games, travelling bags, Christmas decorations, plastic pneumatic toys, and toy animals made of cloth. Most of Taiwan's lamp oil goes to Iran.

CONCLUSIONS

The major headings in any category of products offered for export by a foreign country may contain subheadings that differ considerably from those in any other country. In the case of mainland China, it may be a greater and more inexpensive supplier for you in a product line that no Chinese has thought of since his only market has been a local one. It would be up to you, the buyer, to be clever enough to see either a new application for an existing product and an entirely new market for a modified existing product or for an entirely new type of product.

In Taiwan, on the other hand, you have an aggressive existing and modern production machine made lean and mean by the loss of political "face" but not of its trading acumen. For a quick source, Taiwan is a key-source market for many goods, as for polyester or synthetic-based textile garments. It is obvious from the information in this chapter that for cotton-based goods aimed at the western market, Hong Kong is the better source.

But for the buyer with some holding power, there can be no better future source than China because of its favorable labor-intensive values. Labor costs will have to be subsidized for years by the communist government until China is capable of competing with other exporting nations like Taiwan or ports like Hong Kong.

The United States is the hottest consumer market in the world. By any standard the American market sizzles and is eager for a good deal. When the buyers favor a product, the supplier prospers, sometimes by incalculable profits. The hula hoop of yesterday could be the luxuriously decorated hand-made Chinese kite of tomorrow. The VCR of today may be replaced by tomorrow's version which automatically excludes the commercials and the station signatures.

The differences between the markets we have discussed are remarkable by western measure. The reader will recall that China has 1½ television sets per 100 inhabitants. Taiwan has one television set for every four people, for every hundred people there are 25 television sets, probably full color, too!

The impact of the analogies is not comedy, but the drama of the differences. The greatest unexplored source-market in the world is mainland China. One of the most polished foreign trade colonies in the world will revert to China in 1997. One of the most resourceful exporting countries is next door, Taiwan. All three are in the shadows of the industrial giant, Japan.

These three chapters have focused on one of the most dynamic areas for purchasers to look for mail order products. In a relatively small section of the world are these three vibrant source-markets. It is time to sit back and to reflect, use your imagination and common sense. If you want lace, you would normally look to France for Chantilly lace, or to Belgium with its famous Bruges lace. Lace is a labor-intense product. It can be produced by machine. It does not take magic to understand that China can produce hand-made lace, if asked.

It is time to match up a needed product. An exotic product. A well-priced product.

Marketing

HOUSEWARES, APPLIANCES AND HARDWARE

Hong Kong?

TAIWAN PRODUCTS GUIDANCE monthly

P.O. BOX 68-855 TAIPEI TAIWAN / CABLE "TGPCE" TAIPEI

ALUMINUM/STAINLESS **COOKWARE**

Clocks, Watches, Jewelry and Gifts

TAIPEI TRADE SHOWS

Chapter Five

STEP THREE
How To Write The First Letter To Your Far East Suppliers

Getting yourself established with overseas manufacturers is a relatively simple matter provided you observe certain rules of good business practice. In many cases you will be dealing with relatively large firms, and it is apparent that such firms do not wish to get involved with amateurs, or others who appear to have no chance of becoming good, steady customers.

Most manufacturers are anxious to do business with you, however, if your correspondence with them indicates that you don't know what you are doing and most likely won't develop into a consistent buyer of their goods. Then as a matter of fact, you will be better off not attempting to buy wholesale at all until you have definitely made up your mind that you are going into business and intend to handle a certain class of goods. If you are already established as a retail dealer, of course, then these points will offer nothing new to you.

The first requirement, perhaps the only indispensable requirement, of a new mail order business is a businesslike letterhead. Such a letterhead should tell 1) who you are; 2) where you are; 3) the nature of your business; 4) your telephone number; 5) and your correct mailing address. A few dollars spent on having a professional-looking letterhead prepared for you will decidedly pay off in the long run. To begin corresponding with prospective suppliers without such a letterhead marks you as an amateur or an individual who is trying to "get it wholesale" for his own personal use. In either case, you are not likely to get much response.

The second important rule in getting established with suppliers is this. Always *type* your letters neatly, accurately, and in a prescribed letter form. This may sound trite, but you'd be surprised how much weight an attractively typed letter carries with the people on the other end of the line, especially if you have never met them or had any personal contact with them in the past.

The third rule is: Get to the point quickly. Don't beat around the bush. State exactly what you want, whether it's a catalog, price list, or just information. These people are busy and are more likely to respond quickly to a letter that is brief, to the point, and specific.

The fourth rule is: Make it easy for them to reply. In writing for information about a specific product, or for information of any kind, enclose a stamped, addressed reply envelope.

The fifth rule is: Keep a copy of all correspondence with suppliers. This will eliminate any possibility of future disputes or misunderstandings.

The following is a specimen letter. It is for requesting information on a particular item. You can use the letter as is or modify it to fit your particular situation. At any rate, it is yours to use, and it has been proven to be effective in accomplishing its purpose.

Date

Name of Firm
Address
City, State, Zip Code

Dear Sir:

I am trying to establish a source of supply for (name of product, description, etc.), please send catalog and wholesale price list.

On receipt of catalog and wholesale price list from you, and contingent upon suitable discounts and delivery schedules, we shall be glad to place an initial order.

Should you not be able to supply this item, we would greatly appreciate your referring us to another possible supplier.

Thank you.

Sincerely,

Your name

Catalogs, Catalogs, And More **"Hong Kong"** Catalogs.
Pick The Right Product and You Could Be A Millionaire
Before The End of The Year!

Chapter Six

STEP FOUR
Three Ways To Make
Money In Mail Order!

Now that you have a product that you are going to sell via mail order, I want to introduce you to three ways to make money in mail order.

When you operate a mail order business, the mailman who now brings you bills brings you money. Sales and the profitability of your mail order business work in partnership with the mail system. The mail gets out your offer and the mail brings the orders. All methods of gathering those orders are derived from three ways you use the mail: 1) Magazine or Newspaper Advertisement; money direct-from-ad; 2) Magazine or Newspaper FREE INQUIRY, follow-up with mailing package; and 3) cold direct-mail with your mailing package.

Method One, money direct-from-ad, is familiar to everyone, simplistic, and perhaps the least involved of methods. The proper ad, properly placed, directly results in sales. To be effective, your ad will briefly and convincingly describe the product and/or service offer. Strong copy, appealing illustrations, or both, can be used. The ad will call to itself the attention of your most likely customer, state the price or terms of the offer, and request the customer's order. Your research of the money direct-from-ad method employed by countless numbers of classified or display advertisers should give you numerous ideas as to what style and length of ad copy best suits your business. The ad should be clear, precise, and simple. Remember: it's an offer (irresistible, of course), plainly an offer.

Method Two, Free Inquiry follow-up, operates on a higher level, is less direct, and opens a wider door for higher priced products or books. With Free inquiry follow-up, the proper display or classified ad is placed before the most likely customers as in the money direct-from-ad method. The thrust of the ad differs in that you are just looking for the name of your customer; no money. Indeed, most of the effective free inquiry follow-up advertising doesn't even attempt to sell a particular item or quote a price! It sells the "sizzle" not the steak. The intent of this kind of ad is to sell the credibility of the seller and the type of product or book it sells. It piques interest and tantalizes the customer's curiosity. Or, it convinces the customer that you have what others don't have or can't do. You have something "secret" unique or hard to obtain. Your ad, of course, tells the customer to write for details, literature, and prices.

Method Three, COLD direct mail, is a powerful, and fast, way to sell your products. It allows for the expanded sales promotion of products, and eliminates placement of advertising, and shortens the time between ad placement and the sale. While a well placed ad using the money direct-from-ad method can be effective, it is a "warm" attempt to sell. You are counting on the readership of the ad's vehicle (Magazine) and the magnetism of the ad. The inquiry follow-up method results in a "hot" name, someone you know wants to hear more. The "cold" direct mail method is also a "hot" method. It employs a pre-developed listing of customer names. Such lists are available from a number of sources. There are mailing list houses specifically designed to serve you with names of known mail order product or book buyers. You can buy generalized lists or even very specific lists. If your mail order business sells a product that the general public is going to buy, fine. Testing such a list is like a shotgun for getting your offer to a wide range of buying tastes. But, if your product or book is specialized and of interest to a particular segment of the market, investigate list houses that can research that market and supply the names of those specific buyers.

What you are selling, and the price you are selling it for, may determine what method is best for your success. Beyond the differences of these three methods there are really no additional methods.

Every method employs a means. Every means has an intent which must be accomplished. Every accomplished means of a method has a result. And every result worth going after has a built in additional opportunity. That's the circle that goes around, that is motion, and, in business, that's growth.

In Method One, money direct-from-ad, the method is easily understood. Its method is the classified and display ad (notice: you can use both means. Why place a limit on your results?). The intent of this method, is a well written ad that is properly placed in the circulated medium that is most likely to reach your product's market. Even the most striking ad for the greatest product won't accomplish a thing if you're selling womens clothes through a mens fishing magazine., that's obvious. Spend time researching your customer and understanding what magazine(s) he or she reads, what sections of the newspaper he or she reads. A "Grocery Store" (National Enquirer) newspaper's classified ad department can often give you placement in the section that's best for you. S.R.D.S. Magazine and newspaper directories are available which list all published magazines, their circulation figures, publication frequencies, reader profiles, and the typical nature of articles they print. (Address: S.R.D.S. Directory: Consumer Magazine Rates & Data, 3004 Glenview Road, Wilmette, Ill. 60091, (312) 256-6067). The point is you should want to take proper aim at the marketplace.

The content of the ad, as said before, should be clear, brief, and complete. Praise the product, praise the smartness of the person who buys the product. Point out its uniqueness, its quality, its desireability. State the price or the range of prices your products represent and ask for the order. The simple direction "order now" is often all some people need to set the sale in motion. The research you've done already on advertising or competing products will help you know hwat your ad must accomplish.

The result of the dynamics built in to the money direct-from-ad method is also easily seen: money in your post-office box. Your responsibility once the order has been received should be equally obvious: ship. Never underestimate the power of the quick response. Whether you are marketing a consumable that must be re-ordered or a one-time only item, customer loyalty is the greatest cost-free asset of any business. It's a "plus" to go for no matter what method you use. No one re-orders from a mail order business that seems unresponsive or is slow to ship. You should also understand that a quickly satisfied order results in customer telling neighbor, neighbor telling friend, friend telling co-worker, and so on. The rapid turn-around of order and shipment creates the last step in the method: establishing the next opportunity and keeping the ball rolling. Never undo all you've accomplished to this point by assuming the sale is over when the sale is made.

And always keep the door open. If you have additional products or books to sell, send the information with the product or book. Include a receipt or a note of thanks. Never close the door that was opened by all your efforts.

In Method Two, your means are the ad, the FREE Inquiry, and the follow-up response of mailing sales literature that sells the product. Method Two is more involved, but it also opens the door to more possibilities. Since the Free Inquiry follow-up method produces a "hot" potential customer, the lag time between using this method and the sale is made up for by the quality of the response. The direct-from-ad method limits what you can first tell the customer. Once you have a response with the inquiry follow-up method, the door is open. You have the customer's stated interest and attention. Use this open door wisely to say all you can about your product or book and how you can continue to help the customer beyond the sale.

This method is ideal for the mail order business selling a number of products or books for a range of categories. When your customer states the "hot" interest in replying to your FREE Inquiry follow-up ad, be ready to do your part: the follow-up. If you have selected Method Two for sales, you will have both barrels ready in the form of good sales literature. It may not be a full color catalog, but your follow up will at least include a convincing and personable sales letter, an appetizing listing of merchandise and prices, an order form, and a return envelope. Remember to quickly respond, via First Class Mail, to all your inquiries.

In Method Three, COLD direct mail, you should use the same "mailing package" you are using in method two. Once you have the "hot" lead from a mailing list, you can send the entire package of sales literature, order form, and return envelope. Also be sure to include some indication of what the customer could expect in the way of merchandise choice, variety, and price in the future.

By now you can probably envision the dynamics of each method, the pluses and minuses, and how one plays off the other for differing results, for differing reasons. The resulting step in the dynamics of each method used, each corresponding means which accomplish your intent, is the sale. Method One is quick, from ad to sale. Method Two has a built in time lag of ad-inquiry-your follow-up, and sale, but allows for wider merchandising to "hot" prospects. Method Three is also "hot," but eliminates the placement cost of advertising and allows you the chance of immediate wide exposure of the products or books you offer. A limitation of the number of items you plan to sell or in start-up capital may dictate Method One and that may actually be best for you anyway. If you have a number of items for sale, or a related line of merchandise, the Free inquiry follow-up and direct mail methods will offer more opportunities. No matter what method you choose or what method your endeavor dictates, each of the three methods can result in the final step in the dynamics: repeat business.

Once you have received orders from Method One and Method Three, or even after receiving only inquiries from Method Two, begin to build your own customer (Buyers) list. This is where the sale isn't the end, this is where you keep the ball rolling. With this effort, along with referrals (which can be solicited at any point while using any one of the three methods), you're beginning to build a foundation for the future. Using your growing list, periodically send direct mail style offers to your past customers or once "hot" names. A satisfied customer will buy from a mail order business they've previously experienced with greater certainty than from an unknown business offering nearly the same items. Update your inventory or alter your offer to re-interest the customer.

Replacement of an ad will garner new customers, but a sales brochure to a past customer will skip the ad costs. Thanking a customer for last spring's order while mentioning new items can be a very effective direct mail method of its own.

While there are no hard and fast rules, there are advantages and disadvantages to each method, particularly regarding certain products, prices, and markets. Method One has less cost perhaps (less sales literature), but best suits single item sales (say, in a $10-$19 price range). You'll find the truth in studies that show Method One and Method Two techniques work best seasonally, January through March and August through November. Method Two advertising can be actually less expensive sometimes because it requires less ad copy (and the space you pay for) to tease than it does to sell. This method is also best for hard to describe items or for items in a higher price range (roughly translated to $29-$49). In Method Three strategy, the better the list you use (which also may cost a good deal more), the "hotter" the name. Additional list sources include even ones competitors or other non-related mail order businesses. A good beginning would be to contact the *Direct Mail Marketing Magazine* or the S.R.D.S. Directory of "Direct Mail Consumer Lists".

Additional maneuvers in the dynamics of all three methods can be the inclusion of discounts or coupons to hasten the customer's decision to buy. A few blank lines in your sales literature can request from the customer the name and address of friends or neighbors who might also like to know of your business.

You can begin with one product, employ Method One, and move onto Method Two if you develop additional or higher priced items for your business. Method Three will make itself available to you in short order once you begin name building. The three methods to make money in mail order is a fluid world of dynamics, like a ball going back and forth between two players on a court, but the name of the game is one, the sale.

Chapter Seven

STEP FIVE
How To Start Your
Advertising Campaign

By this time, if you followed steps one thru four, you should have a good idea of the type of product you are going to start your mail order company with. Now I would like to show you how to begin your advertising campaign. To save time and space we are going to mix Program One (product importing and advertising) with Program Two (book publishing and advertising.) As we go along you will see that both programs will use the same type of advertising campaign.

You are now on your way to owning your very own mail order company, something very few people in this country will ever try.

Whatever you have heard or read about advertising I want you to blank from your mind. I want you to start fresh and get the basics, down-pat, before you try your hand at advertising. There are several reasons for this type of teaching, which will be apparent to you as we go along.

Whether you are thinking of running your mail order company as a part-time adventure or as a full-time career, you must develop a very specific advertising strategy.

To facilitate this task, this chapter will identify and isolate the following six functions involved in selling products or books via classified ads.

The first thing you should know is that classified advertising is designed to produce leads (names) not cash (Method Two). I see so many people starting their advertising campaign with ads like the following: For a great little product that will clean your garage, Send $12.00 to A.J. Jones, P.O. Box 765, New York, New York 10788."

That is the quickest way to failure and a sure way to lose a substantial amount of your hard earned money. (Never ask for money in a classified advertisement.) Pick up any issue of Popular Science or The National Enquirer and in the classified section of the magazine you will find mail order companies that are wasting their money. But, it is important to know that there are people in the mail-order business who are making a good living by using classified ads. They will never have a million dollar a year mail order company and maybe they never wanted one in the first place, but they are making a very good living by selling products or books via classified advertising.

If you really want to get into the mail order business by way of classified advertising, I will try and take you through a step-by-step format that worked for me, when I first started in the mail-order business.

Step 1: Write a book about a subject that you are familiar with. Or import a product from the far east or Europe. The book does not have to be lengthy, let's say 80 pages typed with your own typewriter, no need to bear the expense for typesetting. (Writing a book is easier than you think. Please read on.)

There are three steps to selling via classified advertising.

First: Write the book (80 pages or longer) about a subject you are completely familiar with or you can research without too much trouble, such as: Gardening, Losing Weight, How To Make Money in Real Estate, Etc. Or import a product from Hong Kong or Taiwan.

Second: Write a catchy classified ad.

Third: Make up a direct mail package.

First: The classic format utilizes a separate outer mailing envelope, white or brown kraft, traditionaly known as a " No. 9." Included in the envelope should be a business like 11 X 17 four page letter done on white paper with black ink. Next an 8½ X 11 brochure done with pictures of your product on colored stock, yellow or blue, using black ink only. A business reply envelope. And last but not least is the order form 3½X8½ done in one color, black ink on white paper. Now you have the classic format, all you have to do is fill in the advertising copy.

This complete mailing package should cost you no more than 15ᶜ each to have 5,000 printed. If you pay any more than that, your whole program may not work. Remember we are talking about classified advertising.

Now you have the basis for starting a classified advertising program.

Second: To simplify this chapter, let's assume for the moment that you have written the book, eighty pages or more, and you have 500 copies printed, ready to go, sitting in your home. Or you have imported 500 products from Hong Kong. Let's also assume that you have designed your mailing package which includes a No. 9 envelope, an 11X17 four page letter, an 8½X11 color brochure, a one-color order form, and a business reply envelope. The mailing package is also printed and ready for mailing, about 5,000 packages, let's say. All that is left, for you to do, is to write the classified ad and place it in the appropriate publications. (Which I will tell you the names of later.)

Now I know, at this very moment, you are wondering how you are going to write the book, write and design the mailing package, and put the classified advertising into operation, since you are probably not a professional copywriter. I realize that. Don't worry. Further along in the book I will show you how to write your first book and how to write ad copy for your mailing package.

Now I want to show you where to place your classified ad and how many times you should run it in each publication.

Assuming that your book is about "How To Make Money, Buying Real Estate, Gardening," etc. Or your product is for general household consumer use, you should place your classified ad in the following publications:

National Enquirer
600 S.E. Coast Ave.
Lantana, FL 33464

Workbench
4251 Pennsylvania Ave.
Kansas City, MO. 64111

Weekly World News
600 S.E. Coast Ave.
Lantana, FL 33464

Winning
15115 S. 76th E. Ave.
Bixby, Ok. 74008

The Star
730 Third Ave.
New York, NY 10017

Mechanix Illustrated
1515 Broadway
New York, NY 10036

Popular Mechanics
224 W 57th Street
New York, NY 10019

Midnight Globe
535 Fifth Ave.
New York, NY 10017

Popular Science
380 Madison Ave.
New York, NY 10017

Family Handyman
1999 Shepard Rd
St. Paul, MN 55116

American Legion Magazine
700 N. Penn St.
Indianapolis, IN 46206

Mother Earth News
1240 Johnson Ferry Place
Marietta, GA 30067

Moose Magazine
100 E Ohio St.
Chicago, Ill. 60611

Grit Magazine
1240 Johnson Ferry Place
Marietta, GA 30067

Medical Bulletin
535 Fifth Ave.
New York, NY 10017

Third: you should run the ads in every publication twelve months a year. What you must do is build a pyramid and here's how it works. For each $1.00 you spend in advertising you should receive two to three names in the first month and one name in the second month and a ½ of a name in the third month.

So let's suppose you spend $500.00 in advertising the first month and you receive 1,200 inquiries, the second month 450 inquiries and the third month 225 inquires. Out of the 1,200 inquires you received and sent a mailing package to in the first month, let's assume you received 150 orders at $29.95 each. (Assuming again, that you priced your book or product at $29.95.) You have now made $4,492.50 in the first month. Now, since you have paid for the advertising in front, and purchased your products or books and mailing packages with advance payment, your only cost left is postage, 22ᶜ X 1,000 and $1.00 X 150, for the mailing of the mailing packages, and the mailing of the book or product.

Your net profit is $4,122.50.

Do you see now how the pyramid works?

The next step is to take the whole $4,000.00 and spend it for advertising for the next two months, consecutively, $2,000 each month. Don't spend any of it, at this time, on yourself or additional supplies, do that next time (two months down the road).

Now you have created a $54,000.00 a year income which will continue to pyramid into $70,000.00 to $125,000.00 a year over the next three years.

Next part! The percentage of orders from any given 1,000 inquiries is based on several different factors.

First: The type of book or product you are offering.

Second: The publications you are running your classified ad in.

Third: How quick you respond to your customers inquiries.

Fourth: How professional your mailing package looks.

Fifth: Do you have a full four pages of information to sell your potential customers. "Words!"

If you prepare a Professional Looking Brochure in a Professional Looking Mailing-Package, written in a straight forward manner, keeping in mind that you are trying to convince a new potential customer to buy your book or product, you should receive about 8 to 15 returns for each 1,000 inquiries you mail out.

LET me make one point clear!!! This percentage does not apply to all forms of Direct-Mail or Space Advertising. When you get into "Cold" direct-mail and "Full Page" space advertising the percentage changes dramatically.

BACK-END-MONEY! In order to be successful in this business you MUST, I repeat MUST, write a second book or offer a second product preferably along the same lines of your first item.

These items are to be sold as bounce-back sales.

A bounce-back sale is where you place the selling brochure for the second book or product in with the order for the first book or product on its way to the customer. This is where the REAL MONEY is made. In fact about 20 per cent of your customers will order the second item, within two weeks after they have ordered your first item. This is over $5,990.00 of additional income for every 1,000 orders of your first book or product. Assuming your second book or product sells for $29.95.

The Reason that this is so profitable, is because you save the POSTAGE and the COST OF ADVERTISING on the second sale, which is a substantial part of your overall cost of doing business in the classified field.

If I were you, just starting out in the classified advertising field, I would get started on the "bounce-back item" as soon as possible.

To give you an example of what I am talking about, pick out about four or five classified ads in any of the magazines I have recommended. Then send away for their books or products. That way you will get a good feel for the "Back-End-Business."

Chapter Eight

STEP SIX
How To Make a Fast Million Dollars Using "Method Three" Direct Mail

There are 60 million households in the United States as of this date. And let's assume we have picked out a list of 100,000 names to do our test campaign with.

The product sells for $29.95 and costs $5.00 to manufacture, ship to the USA, package, and ship to your customer. This leaves a gross profit of $24.95, which, however, does not take into account the cost of obtaining the order. (Advertising; direct mail) If we feel that the minimum net profit we want to make is $24.95 per item, we can consequently afford to pay $.27 to mail each potential customer on the 100,000 name list. With this cost policy as our guide, let's proceed to the actual mailing.

A mailing consisting of a four-page letter, descriptive 8½ X 11 brochure, order form, and business reply envelope (BRE) is now sent to each prospect on the 100,000 list at a total cost of $27,000 for the first mailing. (15 cents each for printing, and 12 cents each for bulk mailing. $.27 cents times 100,000 equals $27,000. You can start with 10,000 if you like, but for this illustration I am going to use 100,000 names.)

Let's say your response to this mailing yields 5,000 orders, or 5 percent of the list.

5,000 X $29.95 equals $149,750.00 Gross
5,000 X $5.00 cost of product, equals -$25,000.00
100,000 X $.27 cents to mail names, equals -$27,000.00
100,000 X $60 per thousand to rent names, equals -$6,000.00
NET PROFIT $91,750.00

If you do this part of the campaign only, for the next eleven months, you will make a cool million dollars; NET PROFIT.

It is as easy as that, no hidden gimmicks. Just find a good list of 100,000 names, import a product that costs less than $5.00, including shipping and handling, and make up a direct mail package that sells the product.

Another phenomenon of interest is the fact that a follow-up identical to the previous one can be sent to the same list without appreciable decrease in response. Naturally this procedure cannot be practiced indefinitely on the same names; repetition of the mailing once or twice, however, provides a method of eliciting profitable response without the necessity of changing the contents of the mailing, with its corresponding expense. This very phenomenon is observed also in the case of publication advertising, where the identical advertisement may be repeated in the same magazine or newspaper regularly on a profitable cost per order basis. To understand this situation, it should be realized that the first advertising message may be missed for one reason or another by many prospects. These people may see and respond to the second mailing or advertisement; also those nonbuyers who had seen the first message may be persuaded by the second. This often happens when the prospect experiences a need for the product that was not felt during the reading of the first advertisement.

TESTING

Before running a direct-mail campaign, it is frequently advisable to test the effectiveness of various elements of the proposition. By testing their value first, the advertiser avoids spending money on a comprehensive mailing that incorporates weak elements and he correspondingly increases the profit-making possibilities of his undertaking. The more important units that can be tested are price, method of payment, copy appeals, color of stamps and of printing ink, use of stamps vs. printed or metered indicia, type of letterhead, first-class vs. third-class bulk mailing and the mailing list itself. Be certain not to test more than one element in any single mailing, since it will be impossible to determine which element is responsible for the greater pulling power. Once a low-cost test yields the answer to any of these questions, the advertiser can incorporate the successful elements in his entire mailing of 100,000 names, secure in the knowledge that he is running the most effective campaign possible.

There is no rigid rule concerning the number of names to be used for testing a list. Some mailers select 10 percent of a list, while others prefer 20 percent. When 100,000 prospect names, for example, are available, some advertisers test a 10,000-name cross section of 100,000 names, that is, 10 percent of the full list. Other advertisers make a practice of trying as few as 1,000 names from each of several lists rather than taking 10,000 names from a single list.

If initial testing shows success, the next step is *not* to plunge into the circularization of the remaining names in the entire list, for many of these names may be old. It is good practice to take sections of the list—in groups of 10,000 or 20,000, for example—and mail them. As each group pays off, the next group is mailed. By feeling his way carefully in this manner, the advertiser avoids the very pitfalls into which so many inexperienced operators drop.

TECHNIQUES OF TESTING

Two testing techniques are available to the direct-mail advertiser. He can mail his test *in total* to receive an answer to the question, "How much response may I expect when I mail my full 100,000 mailing?" This information is vital because it determines whether or not the proposition is attractive enough to warrant the expenditure for a complete mailing. For example, if the test yields a return of 2 percent, which proves to be unprofitable on a cost per order basis, the advertiser may decide not to proceed with the full mailing on this proposition. Either some controllable element in the mailing is ineffective, (such as price, ad copy, time of the year) or some outside influence (such as a competitor offering the same item) is hostile to the success of the proposition. Since the advertiser does not know exactly which factor is operating against him, he may attempt to find the answer by use of the second techinque—the *split-run* test.

Let's assume that the advertiser suspects the price of his product to be the culprit. Perhaps the price is too high, causing prospects to refrain from ordering. Or perhaps an even higher price will pull just as many orders and enable the advertiser to operate profitably. Once again a small portion of the complete list is selected; this time, however, the test list is divided into two equal parts. One price ($29.95, for example) is incorporated in half of the test mailing, while the competing price (such as $39.95) is offered in the other half. For valid testing, be sure to *alternate* the names in your test group. That is, select every other name from the computer and have them printed on a separate sheet. The remaining names are placed on another. Then send the $29.95 test mailing to those names in the first pile and the $39.95 mailing to the names on the other sheet.

After the split-run test has been completed, response automatically points out the more successful element, which can then be used for the remainder of the entire list.

THE SEASONAL FACTOR

Certain months are more favorable for direct-mail response than others. Returns are affected by the season, holidays, market conditions, weather, the proposition, nature of the product, sensational news breaks, etc. However, here is an *average* course that direct-mail response may take within limitations of the factors mentioned.

October: One of the best months, people are starting to stay inside more because of the cold weather.

November: Still a great month if you mail early in the month.

December: Decline continues a little more because of Christmas holidays.

January: Best month of the year.

February: Second best month of the year.

March: Small decline until the middle of the month, probably because of warmer weather. Pickup after the middle of the month.

April: Leveling off, slightly below the March level.

May: Sharp decline, probably due to approach of warm weather in most of the country.

June: Continued decline.

July: Sharp pickup.

August: Pickup continues.

September: Great month because TV starts new season and people are starting to stay at home more.

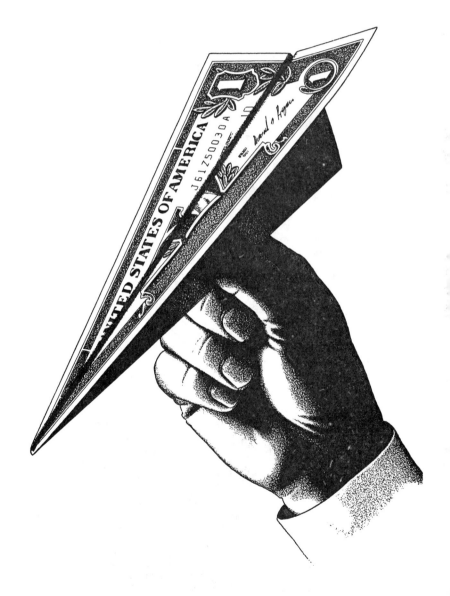

An Invitation

Chapter Nine

STEP SEVEN

"The Credit Part of The System."

Is A Step By Step Plan For You To Make Your First $10,000, $25,000, $50,000, $100,000, and $1,000,000 Dollars In Display Advertising

A misconception which should be dispelled from the beginning is that Direct Mail and Display Advertising are the same. There Are Not! They are as different as day and night!

Direct Mail is a marketing method that utilizes the mail to secure its customers by mailing sales literature in the form of mailing packages. These mailing packages are made up traditionally to include a No.9 outer envelope, a four-page sales letter, a one page brochure, an order form and a white reply envelope. These sales packages are then mailed to the mail order company's potential customers, via either cold mailing lists or a display Advertising program (method two) designed to secure NAMES ONLY, not money, with the order.

Display Advertising or Mail Order Space Advertising, whichever you prefer to call it, is an advertising medium where you are asking for cash in the advertisement and your main purpose, with this type of advertising, is to make the advertisement not only pay for itself, but to make a profit from the advertisement as well.

This form of advertising is my favorite, not just because I made a lot a money from it, but because it is an easier way to get started in the mail order business without investing a large sum of money in the beginning.

COPYWRITING is very important, especially as it applies to display advertising, I have devoted a whole Chapter to the discussion of it.

Let's suppose you have already imported your first product from Taiwan and you have also written and designed your first full page advertisement to market your new product.

Now you are ready to test your first full-page advertisement, let's get started.

The Los Angeles Herald Daily Newspaper is the place to test your first ad. The idea is to test without paying $15,000 thousand dollars to find out if your ad is a winner or not.

Also you want to know the test results right away, not 45 days from now. With the L.A. Herald you can get your full page ad in the Newspaper in three days time and inside of one week you'll have the RESULTS from your first test.

The size for a full page ad in the Los Angeles Herald is 13" X 21". The circulation for the L.A. Herald is all News Stand. The price, at this writing, is about $2,700 for a full page ONE-TIME ad. To purchase the ad you should contact: *Mega Media Associates, Inc., 9555 Warner Ave., Fountain Valley, CA 92708. Please write to Mr. Stuart Cogan first, he is very busy and does not like a lot of telephone calls, unless you are very serious about advertising.*

DAYS NOT to advertise in the L.A. Herald are Saturday and Sunday. Other days NOT to advertise in the L.A. newspaper are December 25th, and April 15th.

"What kind of results am I looking for?" Good question! You are looking for TWO to FOUR times ad cost. If you receive two times ad cost you have a chance with your ad. Make a few changes and test it again in a week. If you receive 3½ to 4 times ad cost you have a winner. Start running your ad in all the Newspapers and Magazines you can find at discounted rates. If you receive 4½ to 5 times ad cost or better, borrow all the money you can lay your hands on. you're on your way to becming a millionaire in the next six months. Don't laugh. It has happened more than once in this business. Run your ad in all the publications I recommend in this book, but only after you have run it one more time in the L.A. Herald just to make sure it wasn't a fluke. (Keeping in mind that your second test should produce 25 per cent LESS

100

than your first test.)

Ok, assume again that you have invested in having your products shipped into this country, and your gross profit is around $5,400.00 ($29.95 each) from your test ad in the L.A. Herald newspaper.

Now you want to PYRAMID your profits into as much advertising as possible. The quickest way to accomplish this is to form your own IN-HOUSE advertising agency. This entitles you to a 15 per cent discount off every advertising dollar you spend. It also lets you access credit.

Let's call this agency the ABC Advertising Agency and lets use your own address and telephone number. (The same one that you are going to use for your MAIL ORDER Company.) You don't have to set up a separate address for the In-House advertising agency, because all of the publishers of the publications, MAGAZINES AND NEWSPAPERS, you will be using, will honor your in-house agency.

Now you want to write to all the publications I have listed at the end of this book and request their display advertising MEDIA KITS. (It should take you about 10 days to receive them in the mail.)

Once you have received them you should make a CHART and list all of their rates, circulation, and lead time. This will enable you to make a comparison of their CPM (cost per thousand). CIRCULATION (News Stand, Paid, or Controlled) and LEAD-TIME for each publication.

Lead time is the time from closing to publishing. Most lead times are either 30 to 45 days in magazines and 3 to 16 days in newspapers. Don't blow the $5,400.00! This is a very important phase of the advertising pyramiding plan. You want to place your ad in as many publications as possible. Don't put the whole $5,400.00 in one publication! Here's what you do.

You make up an advertising insertion order form from your new in-house advertising agency and place an order for a full page ad in all the publications I have listed at the end of this chapter (making sure you send the ADVERTISEMENT and the insertion form together). This should give you about $100,000.00 worth of credit in the various publications, in the following month, which works out to over $200,000.00 income in just 30 days from now. (Assuming you are receiving around two times ad cost.)

I know all of the publications won't accept your proposal, but if half of them do you'll have $50,000 in credit. It's a sure bet that you are better off than if you spend the whole $5,400.00 in one publication and wait for the results.

WARNING! I would NOT try this plan on a untested advertisement. SECOND WARNING! If you fail, you are going to owe the $100,000.00 to the publishers and they will come after you. Also, if they ask for credit references, DON'T fake them, only give them the ones you have on the In-House Advertising Agency (the heart of the credit part of the system) (The printer, sales from your mailing list,, suppliers, L.A. Herald, etc., etc.). Here's where the $5,400.00 comes in. If you are finding that some of the publishers are asking for payment in advance, bargain with them by offering them a partial advance payment and use the $5,400.00 for this purpose. If you're a nice guy and you have been completely honest with the publishers, you will in all likelihood receive about 50 per cent of the credit you have accessed. If for some reason, it hasn't worked out, don't fret. Just start with what you have and pyramid your profits as quickly as possible. You see you can always go back next month with the same proposal to the same publications. Believe me they don't care. They are in business to sell advertising. Besides, next month you will have better credit references because you can now use the publications that did give you credit last month. *Now you are beginning to see how the credit part of the system works. Only the bold survive!* Enough of that, lets get back to business.

I know that their are some of you out there, reading this book, who aren't willing to take such a gamble. That's OK. Each of us follow a different drummer and for those of you who are following a different drummer, I have an alternate plan. Take the $5,400.00 and place one full page advertisement in Mother Earth News Magazine. In thirty days, assuming you are getting at least 2 to 3.5 per cent times ad cost, you should have a gross profit of $11,800.00. After cost of postage, packaging, and a few bad checks, you should have a net profit of about $11,000.00. Now take the $11,000.00 and place it in the following publication: Popular Science

Magazine.

The following publications that I will suggest that you place your advertisements in are full-page ads, always. But, the *Boston Herald* Daily Newspaper is a Jr. page ad, 7" X 10".

I KNOW, I told you not to advertise your product in any less than a full-page ad. But, there are exceptions to everything.

You see, the Boston Herald is a newspaper, tabloid size. So in this case you can get away without paying for a full-page advertisement. In fact, I have found in the past that, if my ad is REALLY HOT, I can make just as much as if I had paid for a full-page ad in the Boston Herald. THIS DOES NOT APPLY to all Magazines or Newspapers, only a few. Which I will point out as we go along.

As you can see, I could go on with this method, about pyramiding for pages and pages. But, by now you should be able to see that the key to Display Advertising is to continually spend your profits in advertising not on your personal bills, or new luxuries. By doing this conscientiously, you will have spent by the end of the season, that comes in April, (assuming you started at the begining of the season in August,) at least $300,000.00 in advertising in the last good month, March. This should, assuming again that you are still getting 3.5 times cost of advertising, bring in over $1,000,000 dollars gross profit.

In Conclsion

Let's go over again what you must do to be successful with the magic nine system, via display advertising.

1. First, you must find and import your first product into this country. Write to all the manufacturers listed in the back of this book; do some research.

2. Write advertising copy for a full page advertisment, keeping in mind to come up with a new and different ad, one that does not look like any other mail order ad.

3. Rewrite your advertising copy five times or six times until you have a winner, (one that produces at least 3.5 times ad cost or better).

4. Form your own in-house advertising agency so you can access the credit and also receive a 15 per cent discount.

5.　Access the credit from all the magazines I have listed at the end of this chapter.

6.　Test your ad in the Los Angeles Herald.

7.　Pyramid your profits into as many full page advertisements in as many publications as you can the following month.

8.　Don't spend the profits on yourself. Put the profits back into full-page advertising.

9.　Don't run in the same publication more than three times in a row. Keep in mind that each time you run in a magazine or newspaper your returns will decrease by 25 per cent.

10.　Months to advertise, in order of best months:

1. January
2. February
3. October
4. August
5. November
6. September
7. December
8. March
9. April
10. May
11. July
12. June

Here is the step-by-step plan for you to make your First $10,000, $25,000, $50,000, $100,000 and $1,000,000 in Display Advertising

This plan is based on the assumption that you are selling a product for $29.95 and your cost to the customer is $5.00. The following publications are in order of preference:
LOS ANGELES HERALD
Full page ad, $2,700 spent, percentage of return 3.5 times ad cost, gross profit $9,450, cost of products, postage and mailing supplies $1,575, net profit $7,875
GRIT
Full page 9 X 12, $7,875 spent, percentage of return 3.5 times ad cost, gross profit $27,562, cost of products, postage and mailing supplies $4,601, net profit $22,961
Place TWO Advertisements Now.
FAMILY HANDYMAN
and
POPULAR SCIENCE

Two full page ads in two different publications, 7 X 10, spent $22,961.00, percentage of return 3.5 times ad cost, gross profit $80,363.00, cost of products, postage and mailing supplies $13,416.00, net profit $66,947.00

This is were you place FIVE ads at one time.

NATIONAL ENQUIRER

MIDNIGHT GLOBE

THE STAR

FAMILY WEEKLY (USA Weekend) West Coast Only.

HOME MECHANIX

Five full page ads, amount spent, $65,000.00 percentage of return, 3.5 percent, gross profit, $227,500.00, cost for products, postage, and mailing supplies, $37,975.00. Net profit $189,525.00.

Here is were you place five more ads at one time.

McCALLS

REDBOOK

PARADE Sunday Magazine (full circulation)

POPULAR MECHANICS

POPULAR SCIENCE (second Time)

MOTHER EARTH NEWS

HOMEOWNERS

NEW SHELTER

SATURDAY EVENING POST

1001 HOME IDEAS

FIREHOUSE MAGAZINE

Total spent $189,000.00, percentage of return 3.5 times ad cost, gross profit $661,500.00, cost of products, postage and mailing supplies $110,434.00, net profit $551,066.00.

At this point I could tell you to bet the whole $551,066.00 on more ads. But, I am assuming you want to start spending some money on yourself, and your family, at this time. So here's what you do. You take $275,500.00 and place more ads. Then take the $275,566.00 that is left and go out a buy yourself a new home and a couple of new cars or what ever you like.

Place $275,500.00 in advertisements in the following magazines. (Some will be the second time around.)
HOME MECHANIX
POPULAR MECHANICS
POPULAR SCIENCE
SPOTLIGHT
NATIONAL ENQUIRER (twice in one month)
MIDNIGHT (twice in one month)
FAMILY HANDYMAN
KIWANIS
ELKS MAGAZINE
VFW MAGAZINE
EAGLE MAGAZINE
MRS. EAGLE
COLUMBIA
AMERICAN WAY
EASTERN AIR LINES
UNITED AIR LINES
EAST WEST NETWORK
AMBASSADOR
KEYSTONE MAGAZINE
MICHIGAN LIVING
1001 HOME IDEAS
NATIONAL MOTORIST
NEW YORK MOTORIST
SUCCESS
SAVVY
HOME AND AWAY

Total spent $275,500.00, percentage of return 3.5 times ad cost, gross income $964,250.00, cost of products, postage and mailing supplies $160,961.00, net profit $803,274.00.

Now you take the $275,566.00 you already have and add it to the $803,274.00 you just made, and guess what, you are now a Millionaire.

WARNING! The two biggest mistakes people make while working "The Magic Nine System" is to go out and hire two dozen people to process the incoming orders. Process them yourself! Yourself and three other part-time people can handle the whole operation.

Second, don't forget to plan your reordering of your products way in advance. Nothing can be more frustrating than to run out of products in the middle of a promotion.

Chapter Ten

STEP EIGHT
A Step-By-Step Plan For You To Become A Great Copywriter

I am going to start out by showing you a step-by-step plan for writing the all important head line and sub head line.
Step One.

THE HEADLINE! It's the most important part of the ad. You must stop the readers from turning the page. Once they have turned the page you have lost them forever.

What should the headline say? Anything you want it to say as long as it leads them, the readers, into the sub head line. You have to look at this part of the advertisement as the start into the greased chute, that will take them (the readers) down and down to the coupon.

The readers are always trying to get lost and find an excuse to stop reading your advertisement. Your job is to prevent that from happening!
Step Two

We're all interested in news. When your new product is of news value, let the headline carry this message by the use of such words as "Now","At Last","How","New", ... "Revolutionary."
Step Three

Tell the prospect that there are several ways to satisfy his desire or several ways in which your product will benefit him.
Step Four

Offer information to readers by stating that you're going to tell "How To" accomplish something.
Step Five

Offer the reader a choice of selection of action by using "Which."

Step Six

Promise to satisfy the reader's desire quickly and easily.

Step Seven

"Amazing" is charged with power if used sparingly. Often the word is combined with "New" to form an effective thought.

Step Eight

When the proposition actually permits, "Free" is by far the best word in a headline.

Step Nine

Begin the headline with "Advice."

Step Ten

Select prospects by beginning the headline with "To."

From a copy viewpoint an advertisement consists of three main elements: headline, sub head line, and body copy. Because of its size and position, the headline may account for as much as 75 per cent of the effectiveness of the entire advertisement. If the headline is not read (stop the prospects dead in their tracks), chances are that the prospect will not read the advertisement at all. It's important therefore that the HEADLINE demands that it be given particularly careful consideration. Three ingredients may be included in the headline's construction, either singly or in combination: attraction of the reader, presentation of the major appeal, and an invitation to read the remainder of the advertisement. Experience has yielded many tested and workable "Steps", shown above, that can be useful in headline creation. However, they should not be employed indiscriminately simply because they have pulled orders for other advertisers. For the best results a formula, of your own, should be united with new raw material from your subconscious mind, resulting in a well-tempered headline.

Naturally these steps are not substitutes for creative effort; an effective headline can be written without their use. However, it is often possible to strengthen a headline by incorporating a tested word phrase. If you believe that using a formula may not exhibit sufficient originality in your copy, then remember that originality in itself should be the major consideration for headline planning.

The goal of every mail-order advertisement is a sale or an inquiry, not a display of the copywriter's brilliance.

THE SUB HEAD LINE

Pick any page of any magazine, and notice what happens after your eye has scanned the headline above the story. Immediately you are confronted with a short sub head line. The sub head line's job is to help the headline and lead the prospect into the body copy. As used in advertising copy the sub head line serves the same purpose and occupies the same position in relation to the headline and body copy. (Never put the sub head line anywhere but between the headline and body copy.) The sub head line must pound-out its theme in hard-selling words and lead the prospect logically into the copy. (Take your time with this part of the greased chute, because this is where you lose 90 per cent of your prospects.) Frequently lack of space does not permit including a sub head line. It then becomes necessary to jump from headline to body copy, the first sentence of which may serve the purpose of a sub head line. In such cases some advertisers set the first sentence in boldface characters or capitals in order to carry the reader more easily from headline to body copy. The sub head line then becomes the first line of the body copy and acts as a bridge leading the reader from the headline to body text and helps sustain the reader's interest.

BODY COPY

The bulk of an advertisement's text is the body copy, following headline and sub head line. This segment of copy offers the advertiser an opportunity to develop his offer, to show the reader how his product can benefit the purchaser, and finally to issue a call for action. The message must be a relatively lengthy one and the body copy must be broken into short blocks by inserting one or two line small sub *body* head lines after every two or three paragraphs.

This improves readability and injects breathing space into what otherwise might be a crowded unattractive advertisement. Another function of these sub *body* head lines is the introduction of a new selling point followed by explanatory copy.

It is a MUST for you to lay out the advertisement so that the headline, sub head line and body copy follow uninterrupted and in logical sequence, refraining from interfering with the reader's progress from headline to the coupon. Therefore when body copy is set with sub *body* head lines, it is a good idea to also CAPITALIZE several key words throughout the copy. This effect will relieve eyestrain and permit the reader to "track-on" to vital words or phrases that otherwise might be buried in the mass of copy.

Two Ways For Writing Copy.

Two copy approaches have proved themselves to be particularly effective in mail-order product selling. The first is the "logical sequence" advertisement technique in which the copywriter proceeds in order from headline appeal down to the coupon. The prospect, at the moment he reads the headline, sub head line, or first paragraph, is not told what the advertiser wants him to do. He learns this after he goes through the body copy and reaches the final paragraph, when he is asked to respond to the offer.

The second technique may be termed the "capsule version" approach in which the entire proposition of the offer is stated immediately in the headline, sub head line and first paragraph. In this case the advertiser feels that the offer —such as a Free booklet, or an unusual money-back guarantee— is of such interest that the reader should learn about it even though he may not complete his reading of the advertisement. The successive paragraphs of the body copy enlarge upon the offer and end in another call for action.

Another successful copy technique departs radically from the approaches mentioned. This is the "reader" type, which closely resembles a NEWS or FEATURE STORY such as the publication might carry. In all cases the product is illustrated, but the coupon is absent, and a personality may appear to be the writer of this type of advertisement.

Tell them all about the product. Or Write a mystery Ad.

Copy can be made more credible by divulging specific facts about the product: exactly how it works, how soon the reader can expect results, and other important specifications the reader may want to know. Product advertising should mention such facts as the product size and the insides (guts) of your product.

Yes, copy should be specific EXCEPT in certain situations. There are occasions when creating a mystery will elicit greater response. Don't tell all; let them guess. This technique works particularly well for the advertiser who is seeking inquiries and is prepared to send follow-up material designed to consummate the sale. The "mystery" approach is also successful when you are selling money making books and are asking for the sale in the advertisement. This type of advertisement will stimulate the reader enough for you to make the sale but remember, don't turn him off because the price for satisfying his curiosity is too high.

Ok, I have given you several types of copywriting. Now, let's assume for the sake of argument that you have chosen the *tell all* advertising method and you are going to charge $29.95 for your product.

This is how you should write your copy keeping in mind that you want it to flow smoothly. You don't want your reader to be knocked off the track and jump to the next page.

A. Headline: You know it must stop the reader from turning the page.

B. Sub Head Line: This part of the ad must lead the reader to the first paragraph.

C. First paragraph: Tell the reader what the product is going to do for him. (Make his or her life easier, etc.)

D. Second and third paragraph: Tell the reader how great the product is.

E. Next paragraph: Assure the reader that this product is not going to cost him a fortune, and that he is not going to have to do any hard work by putting it together, etc., etc.

F. Next paragraph: Tell the start of your story...how you discovered or manufacturered what you are trying to sell him.....how it has worked great for you, how it worked for your friends, how it WILL work fantastically for HIM etc, etc. This part of the advertisement should be a story about yourself and the product. Think of something that happened in your life that caused you to need this product. Keep the story going for about half of the advertisement.

G. Next thing you should do is to bring up information about other people in your life, who you have met, who have profited from this particular product. Also use names of people if possible, then notice how much more readable your ad becomes. TESTIMONIALS from your friends, if you have them in writing, will lend wonders to your copy.

H.   In the next few paragraphs you want to pound home the credibility of your story, keeping in mind that people are interested in THEMSELVES first not you. Try to keep the sentences short. Sometimes words of anger, delight, or excitement will do the job if you use them properly. You must arouse action at this point and get them to the finish line, "THE MONEY-LINE."

I.   Tell the reader that this offer is not going to be available next month or next year. You must offer the OFFER very strongly in the beginning of the advertisement and then take it away. Make them BEG you to sell it to them.

J.   Tell them they have nothing to lose. Tell your prospects the price of your product. This is one of your biggest selling points. "$29.95". You don't know what is going through their minds at this point. They may be thinking you are going to ask them to spend $99.00 for your product. In fact, at this point you should bring up the fact several times that you are only asking $29.95.

K.   Recap all the important parts, reassuring the reader WHAT the product is going to do for HIM. Try to make him feel that if he doesn't order your product he will be missing out on the greatest invention since the invention of computers. Don't be cute. Just hammer-home all the important things that your product will do for HIM.

L.   MONEY-BACK GUARANTEE: This is very important! You must have a very strong money-back guarantee, preferably one that not only guarantees refund for any reason for ninety days, not any less and not any more, which makes all the difference in the world, (when trying to make at least 3.5 times ad cost).

M.   Last but not least! The coupon! Keep the coupon simple. Don't try to make it so complicated that the reader does not know what to do with it. Make it square with dashed lines, never continuous lines and keep it SIMPLE—no credit cards, no COD's, all you want is $29.95 in the form of cash, check or money order. If you want to take credit cards, put in an 800 number or rent one from an telephone answering service.

SECOND PART to the coupon! Please don't forget it. You want to assure the customer prompt delivery. So many times I was all set to order a product from a mail order company, when at the last minute I thought to myself, "HOW LONG IS IT GOING TO TAKE TO GET HERE. The last time I ordered a product from an advertisement like this one it took over eight weeks to reach me." Then your customer is likely to say: "Well, I guess I'll just put this coupon in my wallet and call the mail order company on Monday, when I get to the office, to see how long it takes."

YOU HAVE JUST LOST THE SALE. The customer will never take your coupon out of his wallet and call you. He will forget it and sixty days from now when he is cleaning out his wallet and runs across your coupon, he will throw it in the trash.

By the way, while I am thinking of it, you should always have a telephone listed in the advertisement for questions.

Copywriting can be as easy or as hard as you make it. There is no such animal as a copywriter. There are only people like you and me who practiced and practiced on writing copy. I know you can do it, if you just give it a try. It is not hard once you get going. My advice to you is to write it out using as many words as possible. Don't worry about the spelling at this point. No one is going to read it the beginning stage. Try to incorporate as many of the points that I have showed you.

Here's an idea!

Cut out all the ads in the various magazines and newspapers that pertain to your type of advertising copy. Mark-them-up to see if they are following the same system of writing copy.

Take all of the ads and compare their style of copywriting. (count the number of words in each advertisment. Get a feel for the story in each ad. See how many times they put the price in the ad copy. See how many times they mention the guarantee. See if they offer the reader the opportunity to postdate his check. See if the ad flows smoothly, and most important, see if you are ready to buy after reading the advertisement. This is very important. I know when I finish writing one of my own ads, I'll sit down in an easy chair and place the ad copy in a magazine, like I was reading the magazine for the first time and just ran across my advertisement. I then start reading the ad like it was the first time I ever saw the ad copy. If, when I finish the ad, I am sold, then I know I have a winner. You see, if you can't say to yourself, "Boy, I would buy that product in a minute," and have convinced yourself to buy your product, you can't convince anyone else.

WARNING!!! Don't copy anyone's advertisement! This will finish you before you start. Each ad has a copyright and the owner will put you out of business if you copy their ad. Besides you will never reach your goal by copying other peoples ads.

Readers are looking for something NEW & DIFFERENT and when they find it, they will run to the post office with your order and $29.95 in hand. Believe me, they will!

Before I finish this chapter I would like to leave you with twelve points that will ensure good ad copy:

1. The first sentence should start off with a bang!!!!
Show your prospect that what you are selling will bring him pleasure, or save him money, or increase his knowledge, or better his standard of living.

2. Make an outline of your selling points.

3. Don't start writing copy unless you are in a room by yourself with no distractions, and most important, be in the right frame of mind.

4. Keep the copy moving. Don't stop to rest in the middle of the copy. If you do, your reader will get lost and bored and turn the page.

5. Write your copy like you are writing a letter to a friend. Be friendly but clear and to the point.

6. Don't use words that are jaw breakers. Keep the copy in simple words.

7. Try to inject phrases like:
And.....Now here's the most important part.
And....in addition, you will receive, at no extra charge
Once you read my methods....You will quickly see for yourself
That's not all, You will receive...
But there is one thing more I must tell you...
Take advantage of this opportunity, while it lasts...
For a limited time only I will.....
Send for your copy today, this very minute, while this offer is still in effect.

8. Don't leave the reader puzzled. Tell him exactly what you want him to do.

9. Rewrite your advertisement at least six times, making sure that you have let at least two days pass in between each writing.

10. Create a "PLAY" so when your reader is reading your story, he can picture the places you mention, the people involved and most important keep it current. "Last Year while I was touring America, I found......Two years ago while I was at my friends house in ......Six months ago I discovered..."
Never relate a story that is over two years old.

11. Testmonials....Get your friends to give you some. But, be sure you rewrite them and ask them to endorse your changes in writing.

12. Don't BEG! When you end your copy, just ask for the order and the $29.95. Keep it clear and to the point.

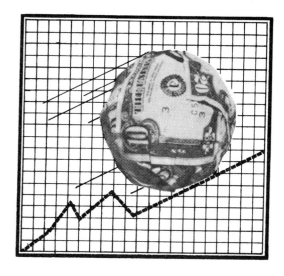

Why Are We Giving Away Famous Nationally Advertised™ MALIN M-15™ SURVIVAL KNIVES for only $4?

Hard to believe, *but true!*

As part of a nationwide advertising campaign, a New York firm will give away one million (1,000,000) of its most expensive hunting knives — the best-selling MALIN-15™ SURVIVAL KNIFE — for the astonishing publicity price of only $4 each to the first one million persons who write to the company address (below) before Midnight, May 31, 1986.

This *original* publicity ad must accompany your request. Copies or photostats are *not* acceptable.

These knives are not copies. These are *genuine* MALIN M-15™ SURVIVAL KNIVES — the same famous survival knives nationally advertised in leading media throughout America. They are the most popular (and most expensive) hunting/fishing/camping knives of their kind ever sold by this multi-million-dollar firm.

A foot long and r-r-r-r-r-r-razor sharp!

If you had to describe the MALIN M-15 in just one word, that word would have to be...*big!* Each MALIN M-15 is a whopping 12 inches long — *a foot in length!* yet so perfectly balanced it cuts and thrusts like an extension of your own hand. Heft this beauty just once; you'll never want to put it down!

Each MALIN M-15 blade is crafted *entirely of 420 molecular stainless!* Thick as a silver dollar at the spine, it's tough enough to split wood or shatter bone. Yet the edge is so wickedly sharp it slices thin as a whisper!

Survival Kit hidden in the hollow handle

But that's not all! In the pommel of each MALIN M-15 is a precision ZF-360 Liquid Damped Compass. And when you un-screw the compass -- there is an aston-ishing Survival Kit complete with packet of waterproof wrapped matches, half-a-dozen fishing hooks, sinkers, nylon test fishing line, sewing needle kit -- even an 18-inch cable saw actually capable of cutting down a a small tree. No wonder this is the best-selling

Compass Unscrews To Reveal Survival Kit

survival knife of its kind ever sold by this multi-million dollar New York firm.

These Famous Nationally Advertised MALIN M-15 SURVIVAL KNIVES will not be sold at this price by the company in any store. There is a limit of two (2) per address at this price, but if your request is made early enough (before May 25) you may order up to five. Each knife is covered by the company's unconditional one-year money-back guarantee.

To get your MALIN M-15 SURVIVAL KNIFE, mail this *original* publicity ad (no copies or photostats) together with your name and address and $4 for each knife. Add only $2 shipping and handling per knife. (New York residents add sales tax.) Allow up to 6-8 weeks for shipment. *Make check payable to CVP Co.* Mail to: CVP MALIN M-15, Dept. 191-102 , Box 1201, Westbury, New York 11595. (V22830)

FREE Sheath & Sharpening Stone If you respond before May 25

Heavy duty sheath for your belt is 1-foot long with lanyard. 6-rivet construction haft retainer, and built-in snap-pouch for sharpening stone (stone included)

© 1986 PDM Inc 1200 Shames Dr Westbury N Y 11590

"This is an ideal advertisement. Large picture of product. Low price. And they ask for more than one order."

118

New! EYE-LEVEL BRAKE LIGHT Gives <u>YOUR CAR</u> 1986 STYLING and SAFETY!

FITS ALL CARS (sedans, coupes, hatchbacks, station wagons), VANS, PICKUPS—ANY YEAR, ANY MODEL—AMERICAN or IMPORTED, with 12 volt system.

Astonishing Fact: Rigid testing by the federal government proved that the third brake light—mounted and functioning at eye-level to following drivers—**reduces rear-end collisions by 53%.**

Astonishing Fact: predictions by the National Highway Traffic Safety Administration (NHTSA) estimate that the eye-level third brake light will **prevent 900,000 rear-end collisions** a year.

Astonishing Fact: Estimates by the NHTSA predict that the eye-level third brake light will **prevent 40,000 personal injuries** a year.

Astonishing Fact: Use of the eye-level third brake light can reduce vehicle damage and repairs by almost 60%.

The overwhelming benefits of the eye-level third brake light demanded strong government action. So in the public interest...

Federal Safety Regulations Now Require Eye-Level-Mount Brake Lights On All 1986 Model Cars.

You owe it to yourself, to those who ride with you, and to those who drive behind you, to equip your car with this light as soon as possible.

Here's How It Works

Your third brake light is mounted at eye level, so it is highly visible to the driver behind you... and to the second and third drivers behind you too!

THIS YEAR'S MOST IMPORTANT AUTOMOTIVE ADVANCE

Third Brake Light Mounts at Eye Level To Instantly Demand Attention

Brilliant Red Light

Drivers following you enjoy improved depth perception...night and day...and tailgaters are warned to keep a safe interval.

A built-in logic circuit is programmed to turn on this light with your car's regular brake lights/and **with your brake lights only**—and that is very important...

This light is coordinated with your brake lights, and positioned in the center of your car, so that drivers behind you cannot confuse it with turn-signal or tail lights...even for a moment.

Installation of this light may even qualify you for a discount on your auto insurance.

Easy Do-It-Yourself Installation

Your light mounts easily INSIDE your rear window—just like new cars—where it is protected from harsh weather, car washes, theft and vandalism. No need for any nasty drilling into your car body. NO wire cutting, stripping or taping either. Special splices are included to let you connect light wires to your brake-light wires...instantly...with any pliers!

Fits ALL Cars, Trucks, and Vans

The universal mounting bracket, pivoting joints, and extra mounting extension make it easy to position your light perfectly. You will enjoy easy installation in any sedan, hatchback, station wagon, pick-up truck, van, or any other American or imported vehicle with a 12-volt electrical system. Your light has a big 6¾" wide x 1⅜" high red lens, and wiring, splices and easy-to-follow illustrated instructions are included.

Satisfaction Guaranteed

J.C. Whitney & Co. stands behind every brake light we sell. Each light comes with our iron-clad promise to you: **Complete Satisfaction or Your Money Back.** If you are not completely delighted with your brake light...for any reason...simply send it back, and we will cheerfully replace it, or promptly refund your money, whichever you prefer.

We believe every car on the road should be equipped with an eye-level third brake light. So we are making them available now...for only **$8.95** each, plus only **$1.00** for shipping your brake light anywhere in the United States. At this low price, you can order one now for every vehicle you own.

Order Today—Delay May Be Serious When split-seconds can save life and limb—and reduce property damage too—it pays to have an eye-level brake light in your car. **Get this valuable protection for your car now.** Simply fill in the coupon below, and send it in with your check, money order, or credit card information.

VISA or MasterCard customers welcome. Simply phone (312) 431-6102... Call 24 hours a day, 7 days a week. Order stock number 81—2289R.

FAST, EASY INSTALLATION... FITS ALL CARS, TRUCKS & VANS

Bright red light turns on only when you press your brakes, so it's impossible to confuse with your turn-signal or tail lights.

Extra mounting extension included...assures easy, perfect positioning in station wagon, pick-up, any vehicle

CHARGE IT WE ACCEPT VISA or MASTERCARD ORDER BY PHONE **(312) 431-6102** 24 hours-a-day—7 days-a-week

J.C. WHITNEY & CO. • 1917-19 Archer Ave. • P.O. Box 8410 • Chicago, IL 60680

COPYRIGHT · 1986 WARSHAWSKY & COMPANY dba J C WHITNEY & COMPANY

JC WHITNEY CO.
Established 1915
1917-19 Archer Ave.
P.O. Box 8410
Chicago, IL 60680

☐ **YES!** Please send me (quantity) _____ No 81-2289R Brake Lights at $8.95 each plus $1.00 each for shipping (United States, its possessions, A.P.O. and F.P.O. only). Illinois residents add 7% sales tax. Chicago residents add 8% sales tax.

☐ **FREE!** One-year subscription to J.C. Whitney's famous Catalogs

☐ I enclose check or money order for $ _____
☐ Charge to my VISA or MasterCard

Expiration Date _____

Card Account Number _____

Signature (Needed only if charging order) _____

Name _____

Address _____

City _____

State _____ ZIP CODE _____ Code [EGYN]

"This advertisement is layed out very well. Large headline, super sub head line, and good picture of product.

"This advertisement is the best. Large picture of product. Lots of illustrations on how to use the product. Large, catchy headline."

120

Chapter Eleven

STEP NINE
How To Write
Your First Book, Even If
You Can't Type or Spell

Writing a book is a lot different than writing ad copy. You can write your book on any subject, in any style, in any size you like. (8½X11 or 5½X8½ are the two most popular sizes.) Keep in mind that you are not trying to sell somone something you are trying to provide information and pleasure.

Writing a book can be easy and a lot of fun, if you get started NOW. Don't wait for the moon to be in the right place. And don't wait until you "feel" just right. No one in this business, gets that " Magic"feeling.

They just Start.

Start Now!

Here's how it is done!!!

Pick a subject, any subject. " Let's seeeeee, here's one. *How To Get Rich!* I bet everyone is interested in how to get rich."

Now that you have the subject, you must do some research. Start out by going to your local library and checking out every book on How To Increase Your Income, How To Buy Real Estate with No Money Down, How To Make Money In the Stock Market etc, etc. Second, send for every book that you see advertised in various men's Magazines, Newspapers, and TV. The get rich books, you know the ones I am talking about. You see them advertised in all the opportunity and financial publications. Buy every one you can lay your hands on. Then go to your local book store and purchase every book about your new subject—money making.

Next start subscribing to every Newsletter, Magazine or Periodical that has anything to do with money making.

Read everyone of them and everything you can find that pertains to Making Money, Investing Money or just plain Money. It should take you about thirty days to read and subscribe to all these publications and books, if you stick to it and START NOW!

Now you are ready to start writing your first book! Please..... don't get turned off at this point. You have just become an expert on the subject of making money and how a normal everyday person can increase their income. You should write a book about it. You owe it to the world and you owe it to yourself.

Easier than you thought?

Ideally, you would like to write approximately 110 to 160 pages. *"Don't get cold feet now."* You're on your way to making a fortune selling books. Don't let your mind tell you it isn't worth it. It is worth it. Just keep reading this chapter and I will show you how easy it is.

Here's How To Write Your First Book, without being able to type or spell.

First. Subscribe to "Writers Digest!" It's a magazine that contains one of your keys to your new future and your new fortune. The address is: 9933 Alliance Rd. Cincinnati, Ohio 45242.

At the end of this chapter I have listed several people and companies that will type your manuscripts from the cassette recording.

Second. Once you receive a copy of the magazine look in the back and you will find about two dozen typists who will type your manuscript from your cassette tape recordings. The charge for this service is very inexpensive and the best part is they can Spell, Punctuate and have a gift for Grammar. Establish a rapport with one of them and send your first tape to them for typing. Tell them that they have a free-hand to make any changes in your recording that may improve your writing skills. Pay them a little more if you have to, but let them add a few verbs here and there or just let them flower it up a little.

I know....I know!

You can't wait until it comes back!

You won't believe what a fantastic writer you have become in just one short week. The next thing you know, you will start thinking: One Hundred Thousand sold the first year.....times $12.95 is ??????

I know!..... I know! We all go through it. Come on, get off cloud nine and get back to the tape recorder. Keep talking! Keep talking! Don't stop. If you stop, for a week or two, you will find it very difficult to finish your book. Keep going, push yourself.

If all goes well, it should take you about thirty days to finish it, even if you only spend a few hours every evening working on it.

Ok, let's assume for the moment you have finished your first book and you have just mailed the last tape to your typist for typing. Assume once again, that you dictated between 100 and 160 pages of material.

Now your manuscript is ready for typesetting.

Always have the book typeset. If you should decide to distribute them in libraries or book stores you will find they won't accept them if they are not typeset.

Next, you should subscribe to a clip art service. There are a lot of them to choose from, but I think I have found one of the better ones in the country:

Dynamic Graphics

6707 N. Sheridan Road

Peoria, Ill. 61614

Telephone 309-691-0428

Dynamic Graphics has a service whereby they provide you with Art Work which you can use to make your book more interesting by inserting pictures or drawings in each chapter. This does wonders for the book and lends credibility to your writing. Besides it will make it much more interesting for your customers to read.

Ok, Now you are ready to have your book printed. The biggest mistake most new authors make at this point is to have a local printer print their new book. You can't afford to have a local printer charge you $5.00 per copy and you in turn sell it for $12.95. You will never make any money that way.

You must seek out TOP Quality Printing for the lowest possible price. In addition to that, you must have the book typeset and the standard price for this service is $8.50 per page.

Surprise!!!

I know someone who will typeset your book for FREE!!!

The name of the company is Maverick Publications in Bend, OR. Their telephone Number is 503-382-6978. Call them and ask for their typesetting and printing rate card. Of course they will want to print it for you at the same time, but this isn't a bad deal because their prices are fairer than most and a lot cheaper than your local printer. If I remember correctly they charge $1.50 per book, typesetting included. This is for the ideal mail-order book 5½ X 8½ paperback, starting out with about 500 copies.

WE ARE THE CHILDREN

Special Offer

ONLY $5.00
FOR 2 AUTHENTIC "CHILDREN OF THE WORLD" DOLLS™

YOU GET 2 DOLLS – ONE BOY, ONE GIRL.

As part of a worldwide awareness program—we will offer 2,000,000—famous Children of the World Dolls for just $5 for a boy and girl doll—that's right . . . you get two not just one . . . but both for this incredible low price. No gimmicks . . . no closing dates. Just $5 until the supply runs out. . . .

Each lovable doll comes complete with its own personal birth certificate registered with the Children of the World Society.

*Each doll is fully dressed in the rainbow colors representing all the nations of the world (machine washable).

To obtain your 2 dolls, fill out coupon—orders will be filled as received. 30 Day Money Back Guarantee if not delighted.

*Each doll is approx. 11" tall and each is clothed in decorative dress—they have soft muslin bodies and wipeable faces. Dress and Size may vary.

Do not confuse this doll offer with any look alikes. This is the only Children of the World Doll offer.

· World Dolls 1985

"This advertisement is weak on copy and the headline does not say anything."

125

"This advertisement looks all right, but I would have elected to use a cheaper product in my space advertising program, and used this more expensive product as a back-end sale."

New Technological Breakthrough

HOW TO UNLEASH YOUR MIND-POWER TO ACHIEVE ALL YOUR GOALS FASTER.
Subliminal Stimulation™ is Today's Answer. It's NEW!

You've read in science and technical magazines about the great success of subliminal stimulation™ techniques. Now, thanks to recent breakthroughs by leading scientists, you can use these same innovative techniques to step up your accomplishments and unleash your mind-power!

For example, maybe you want to sharpen your memory. This is really important when you're working on your car or building things around the house. There are so many steps to remember. Or maybe you need to lose weight, stop smoking or hone your mental skills. Just think how great it would be to grab money-making opportunities by drawing on your mental capabilities to the maximum extent. Or maybe you want to lessen stress, have greater self-esteem and razor-sharp decisiveness. These are just a few of the accomplishments now easily within your grasp.

The subconscious or "inner mind" is a mysterious thing. Scientists are finding out more about it every year. It's not like your conscious mind. Instead it soaks up impressions. You'll be amazed how fast the "success-mechanism" already within you will put you ahead of the game in life.

Subliminal Techniques are men's problem solvers for the 1980's and beyond.

Subliminal stimulation is a remarkable scientific discovery. For example, to reduce shoplifting. Department store managers nationwide are finding that a "hidden" message in the public-address music cuts pilferage substantially. This message repeats over and over such tested phrases as "I am honest. I don't steal."

Talk about effective! Customers aren't even aware of it. Yet inventory statistics prove there's a big decrease in shoplifting. In fact, in some cases by as much as 67 percent.

Your subconscious is powerful. Put it to work to bring you success fast. Thousands of men already are.

Until recently, scientists were stopped dead in their tracks in figuring out how to harness the powers of the inner mind. For years we've known it could be tapped. But the big question was: "How can the average man put its huge power to work?"

Through constant testing a breakthrough finally came. The credit goes to some of the top scientists in the country. Their hard-hitting efforts now enable you to push ahead, no matter your goals, and enjoy tremendous success fast.

The answer is Subliminal Stimulation Tapes. Each brings you two different kinds of assistance.

Put a tape on your regular cassette player—then get ready for a surprise. On one side is subliminal stimulation™. Here's how it works: You hear waves breaking on a rugged shoreline. But your subconscious hears more. There are subliminally embedded messages at work—literally hundreds. Now you'll have a hard time hearing them consciously. But your subconscious will hear them as clear as a bell. Scientists have found the subconscious then goes into gear at once.

Listen while you work around the house or while relaxing, watching TV or even while jogging, working out, or driving your car. The sounds of the waves make a smooth background while alone or with your family or friends.

Subliminal stimulation is so effective it's being featured in scientific and technical journals. Just wait until you try it! It's a totally new, yet natural, experience. You'll feel at home with it fast. A to-the-point briefing on each tape gives you the exact wording of the subliminal messages coming up. It's really fascinating and worry-free.

Now, on the other side you'll hear a voice. This is called the natural response™ program. You'll hear "commands to your subconscious." Think what it will mean to actually be in control of your subconscious. At last, you'll be showing it who's boss!

Be a part of the cutting edge of today's world of science.

Here's your opportunity to discover a sure-fire way to achieve all your goals—no matter what they are—in record-breaking time. You'll feel more alive, more virile and see success after success come your way. Taking advantage of new scientific discoveries puts you one step ahead of the crowd.

Professionals nationwide are finding Subliminal Stimulation Tapes to be one of the biggest scientific breakthroughs of the 80's. Each side actually wakes up your inner mind. Result? You'll see yourself becoming sharper, more "in charge" than ever. You'll get more done faster. And the great part is, each side is so relaxing you'll want to listen time and time again.

Don't let your subconscious lay idle. Put it to work. Scientific-minded men everywhere are—with outstanding success.

Order today. Read about this Special Money-Saving Offer:

Each Subliminal Stimulation™ Cassette sells for $14.95. But during this Special Introductory Offer to Popular Mechanics readers, the price is only $9.95. You save $5.00 on each and every selection.

But here's still more good news. You get one FREE for every three you order! Just fill out the No-Risk Express Order Form and rush it back today, along with your check or money order. Or use your Visa or MasterCard. You're protected by our FULL MONEY-BACK GUARANTEE: We call it our "triple-length" guarantee because it's good for 90 days, not 30. If you're not elated with the results the tapes bring, return them for a full, prompt refund—including the $2 shipping and handling.   1985 Advanced Learning Systems, Inc.

"This advertisement needs a picture and a better headline."

127

Chapter Twelve

Untapped European Resources

F. Lli Moretti s.d.f.
Via Corsica 14 - P.O. Box 86
I 25066 Lumezzane Renzo (Bs), Italy
Casting of artistic and nautical gift in brass.

GERZ GmbH
D-5411 Sessenbach, West Germany
Stoneware Factory for Beersteins and
Dinnerware

D'IRIS di Ferraioli Cristina
S.S. Paullese Km 27
I-26010 Monte Cremasco (Cremona), Italy
Notions: Thimbles, knitting needles, crochet
hooks, twine holders.

Wade of England
Wade Potteries Limited
Greenhead Street
Burslem, Stoke-on-Trent,
Staffs. ST6 4AE, England
Ten of Disney's most loveable creations in
hand decorated porcelain.

Enlite Engineering Ltd.
P.O. Box 24
Haslemere, Surrey, England
Football lampshade.

Alfred Walther
Martinlamitz
D-8676 Schwarzenbach, West Germany
Bells and gongs as used in the Alps.

August Anzmann GmbH
P.O. Box 101426
D-8900 Augsburg 1, W. Germany
Rosaries and other religious articles.

Zeta Studio D'Arte SNC
Via Oberdan n. 10
I-60022 Castelfidardo (AN) Italy
Gift articles in 24K gold laminate, 925/000
silver laminate and 23K gold leaf, 925/000
silver laminate statuettes.

Alfred Auth KG
P.O. Box 1146
D-5880 Luedenscheid, West Germany
Cigarette cases, tobacco boxes, cigarette
rollers, pocket ashtrays, powder compacts
and pillboxes.

Otto Mattuck
Post Office Box 48
D-6955 Aglasterhausen, West Germany
Smokers' utensils.

Alfred Starck GmbH & Co.
Schmuckwarenfabrik
P.O. Box 1767
D-7530 Pforzheim, West Germany
Manufacturers of goldplated metal, silver
and gold ladies jewellery, cuff-links and
men's jewellery.

Ruggero Celli
16, Via Venini - I-20127 Milano, Italy
Smart jewelry, knick knacks, gifts, pewter
and toys.

APA Giovani S.r.l.
P.O. Box 190
I-80059 Torre Del Greco/NA - Italy
Corals and Cameos

KB Uhren GmbH & Co. KG
P.O. Box 200, Predigerstrabe 52
D-7210 Rottweil/Federal Republic of
Germany
Clocks and movements manufacturers.

Herbert Richter
D-7540 Neuenburg
P.O. Box 24, West Germany
Clock factory.

Succ. F.Ili Unger di Rossi
20, Via S. Maria Fulcorina
I-20123 Milano - Italy
Finished costume jewelry.

Manfred Raisch GmbH
3 Ebereschenweg
D-7530 Pforzheim-Buechenbronn,
West Germany
Mechanical alarm clock.

Uariata
D. Lang Kisslingweg 50
D-7130 Muhlacker West Germany
Produces metal articles as frames for
cosmetic bags, evening bags and for the
leather-goods industry, metal accessories,
metal-mesh bags, metal-mesh-belts and
metal-mesh ties, Bell Pull Hardware and
also embroidery kits.

TRE B srl
10-12, Via Reggio Emilia
I-20094 ASSAGO/MI, Italy
Classic-style clocks.

Adrista Ltd.
Adrista House, Unit One,
Sandford Lane Industrial Estate
Sandford Lane, Wareham,
Dorset BH20 4Dy, England
Selection of necklet clasps and findings.

Rosemarie Feld
Krawattenfabrication
Postfach 973, 4150 Krefeld
Ties and scarfs

Elza GmbH
P.O. BOx 1136
D-8078 Eichstaett, West Germany
Carnival and fancy costumes, net gloves and
hosiery, bathing dresses.

Progressive Enterprises Ltd.
Export Division 131 High Street
Sliema - Malta
Handmade silk ties, bow ties, knitted ties,
imitation leather ties, school or club ties
with logo, ascots, cravats, scarves.

Rudi Emmerling KG
P.O. Box 265
D-8450 Amberg, W. Germany
Specialists for Bridal Veils.

Manifattura IDEAL
2/4, Via Bernasconi
I-22029 Uggiate / CO - Italy
Hand-painted quilts and spreads, chintz
cushions.

MA-PLAST
150, via Castelleone
I-26100 CREMONA - Italy
Plastic refrigerator bags and units, beach
and shopping bags, swim rings, sponge
rubber gloves, shower caps, tablecloth and
coaster sets, wallets, record, cassette and
tape boxes, garment bags, and lots more.

Johann Becker GmbH
Postfach 1004 - Industriestr. 12
D-6451 MAINHAUSEN 1
Fed. Republik of Germany
Evening bags.

August Buenger
Bob-Textilwerk
P.O. Box 240180
D-5600 Wuppertal 2, West Germany
Specialists in curtain, net and home textile
accessories.

Indu-Miljo Randers A/S
Messingvej 40
DK-8900 Randers, Denmark
Health mattress Im-Sulate

John Corby Ltd.
28 Frances Road,
Windsor, Berkshire, England SL4 3AD
Classic English trouser press.

Goettman Caps & Hats
P.O. Box 62
D-6140 Bensheim 1, West Germany
Caps and hats for sports and casual wear.

FinnComfort GmbH
P.O.B. 48
D-8437 Freystadt, West Germany
Shoes.

AB Ernol
P.O. Box 126
S-33027 Hestra, Sweden
Clothes hangers, clothespins and towel
holders.

Staude & Co. KG
D-8922 Peiting, West Germany
Leather watchbands.

Robinclay Ltd.
Maple Walk, Bexhill-on-Sea
East Sussex TN39 45N, England
The Bonfit Patterner.

Bali-Buesten
Manufaktur GmbH
4 Buschdorfer Str.
D-5300 Bonn 1, West Germany
Dressform.

Elda Originals
188 Finchley Road, London
NW3 6DR, England
Sensational NO BRA.

Soves S.r.l.
26, Via Cornalia
I-20124 Milano - Italy
The Greenrose Beauty Box system:

Heldt & Co.
P.O. Box 11809,
D-4980 Bunde 1
West Germany
Beauty supplies.

Giesen & Forsthoff
P.O. Box 100824
D-5650 Solingen 1, West Germany
Scissors.

H. G. Junemann GmbH & Co.
Salzerstrabe 1
D-3582 Felsberg/Eder
West Germany
Articles for care of hair and hair grooming.

Gebr. Karscholdgen
P.O. Box 110527
D-5650 Solingen 11, W. Germany
Solingen scissors.

Malteser-Stahlwarenfabrik
Willi Bals (KG)
P.O. Box 100566,
D-5650 Solingen 1, W. Germany
Manicure Display Cabinet M 5023 including
106 pcs. care implements.

August Henning GmbH
P.O. Box 1960
10 Henkestrasse
D-8520 Erland, West Germany
Cosmetic bags.

Konsumex
Budapest
P.O. Box 58
H-1441 Budapest, Hungary
Helia-D

Paul Losenbeck KG
P.O. Box 110708
D-5650 Solingen 11 (Ohligs), West Germany
Scissors and manicure implements.

Ivalda S.P.A.
36, Viale dell'Industria
P.O. Box 179
I-36016 THIENE, Vicenza, Italy

Herder Manicure
D-5650 Solingen 17
P.O. Box 170150

Cons. Ar. For.
9/A, Via Luigi Ottolina (Loc. Scarenna)
I-22033 ASSO / CO - Italy
Scissors.

Kuno Moser GMBH
P.O. Box 20
D-7731 Unterkimach, W. Germany
Electric shavers.

TITANIA-Fabrik GmbH
Krupp-Str. 41-45
D-5603 Wulfrath, FR Germany
Nail and foot files.

Do. Tobell'
Via V. Veneto, 21
36016 THIENE - Vicenza (Italy)
Corn-plasters, deodorizing insoles.

Stohr AG
CH-9602 Bazenheid, Switzerland
Cindy hair care accessories and hair
ornaments.

Georges Marchand Ltd.
CH-2738 Court, Switzerland
Maniquick, battery-operated nail file.

A. & W. Goddert
II. Heidberg 26-27
D-565 Solingen, FR Germany

Electrulux-Kern GmbH
Sanamat Export Office
11 Tucholskystrasse
D-6000 Frankfurt/M. 70, W. Germany
Line of health care appliances, belt and
hand massagers.

Emil Kranzlein AG Brush Manufacturers
P.O.B. 1360
D-8520 Erlangen, Germany
Complete brush sets: hair, bath and nail
brushes, cosmetic brushes, baby brushes,
brushes for technical purposes.

Metronic Electronic GmbH
P.O. Box 382
22 Rheinwaldstr.
D-7210 Rottweil, West Germany
Electrostimulation appliance for
electrotherapy.

Hermann Haag & Sohn
D-555 Bernkastel-Kues
P.O. Box 1205, Germany
Sapphire Nailfiles.

Pharmadrug
P.O. Box 680260
2000 Hamburg 65 Germany
Antatets.

Steinbruck & Drucks GmbH
P.O. Box 100164
D-5650 Solingen 1
Pedi-corn cutters.

Swiss Brush Ebnat-Kappel Ltd.
CH-9642 Ebnat-Kappel, Switzerland
Hairburshes, dental care products, articles
for personal case and massage and shaving
brushes.

La Mobilbagno S.r.l.
Strada per Castelletto
I-20080 Albairate /MI - Italy
Bathroom accessories.

Deco Lampen BV
P.O. Box 178
NL-1970 AD Ymuiden, Holland
Lamps and lampshades, gift articles.

Kurt Bork, Inh. A. Bork
P.O. Box 1268, 4 Hexengasse
D-8867 Oettingen/Bavaria, West Germany
Dolls in national costume.

Elasto Form
Gerhard Sperber
P.O. Box 446, Am Hagen 19
D-8562 Hersbruck, West Germany
Coloured plastic bags.

Velo Schauff
P.O. Box, 548 Remagen, West Germany
Tandem bicycles.

Vereinigte Pinselfabriken
Leonhardy & Co. OHG
41 Johannisstrasse
D-8500 Nuernberg, West Germany
Artists' brushes.

Carnival Toys s.a.s.
di Minghetti Pietro
9, Via Piave
I-48010 GODO / RA - Italy
Carnival and party masks, toys, gags,
"dress up" gear.

GIO PLAST, S.r.l.
4, Via Finale
I-20092 Cinisello B./MI, Italy
Toys, soap bubbles, Western kits, practical
jokes, puzzles, yo-yos, toy arms, summer
holiday articles.

ADF
Via Tagiura, 23
20145 Milano, Italy

Heim-Electric Export-Import
Haus der Elektroindustrie
6 Alexanderplatz, GDR-1026 Berlin,
German Democratic Republic
Sound and video equipment.

Hans G. Hasselbusch
P.O. Box 130231
D-5650 Solingen 13, West Germany
Optical magnifiers.

Ritter GmbH
1 Frankenstrasse
D-8752 Moembris, West Germany
NC rechargeable flashlights.

Adolf Hanhart
Uhrenfabrik GmbH & Co KG
D-7730 Villingen-Schwenningen
Postf. 3247
Hanhart stopwatches.

Rufflette (Export) Limited
Sharaston Road
Manchester M22 4TH, England
Functional motoring accessory products.

AccuLux Witte & Sutor GmbH
P.O. Box 1140
D-7157 Murrhardt
Garden and cultivation novelties.

Landmann GmbH & Co KG
P.O. box 770270
D-2820 Bremen 77, West Germany
Barbecues and accessories.

Eurocamping di Patuzzo V.&C. S.a.s.
32, Via S. Nicola da Tolentino
I-25066 Lumezzane Pieve (Bs) Italy
Gas-cyclinders, grills, lamps, stoves,
camping articles.

Weihrauch Sportwaffenfabrik
D-8744 Mellrichstadt, Germany
Air guns, pistol, gas and alarm weapons,
revolvers for sport and self-defense.

Rodel Modellbau-Technik
D-8939 Ettringen
Radio controlled aircraft model building
kits.

Uniflame s.r.l.
6, Via de Marchi Gherini
I-20128 Milano, Italy
Portable stoves and lamps.

Webley & Scott Limited,
Frankley Industrial Park
Tay Road, Rubery, Birmingham B45 0PA
England
Airguns.

Kronpreis
Metallwaren GmbH
Industriegelande 2
D-8357 Wallersdorf
Sports trophies and awards.

Regal Style Srl
54, Via Roma
I-15040 Mirabello Monferrato / AL, Italy
Gift articles and tableware in brass, silver
and 24 Kt. gold plated.

Credo-Stahlwarenfabrik
Postfach 22 02 6 1
5650 Solingen 1, W. Germany
Kitchenware.

Fratelli Piazza S.a.s.
I-28023 Crusinallo / NO Italy
Stainless steel products.

Karo-As Cutlery
Richard Abr. Herder GmbH & Co. Solingen
P.O.B. 100867
Rathausstrabe 22,
D-5650 Solingen 1,
Frosteese Ultra household knives.

Probus Kitchencraft
Mere Green Road
Sutton Coldfield, West Midlands
B75 5BX, England
Quality kitchen products.

Ruffoni
P.O. Box 11
I-28026 Omegna / NO, Italy
Solid copper with brass handles.

Besana Materie Plastiche s.r.l.
123, Via Lodovico il Moro
I-20143 Milano - Italy
Cocktail picks, toothpicks, salt and pepper
sets, dishes for grated cheese.

Karl Bahns
Stahlwarenfabrik
Burger Landstr. 60
D-5650 Solingen 1, West Germany
Cutlery.

Carl Schmidt Sohn
P.O. Box 100748
D-5650 Solingen 1, West Germany
Flatware.

Fernhurst Ltd.
140 Newington Rd., Ramsgate,
Kent CT12 6PR, England
Domestic electrical appliances, including
plastics injection moulding.

Sherriff Textiles Ltd.
The Praze, Penryn, Cornwall,
TR 10 8AA, England
Aprons, bags, kitchen co-ordinates.

Calderoni F.Ili Italy
I-28022 Casale Corte Cerro
(Novara) Italy
Cutlery.

Hofmann GmbH
11 Kreuzstrasse
D-6983 Kreuzwertheim, West Germany
Multispice shakers.

Rigamonti Pietro & Figli snc
6, via G. B. Moroni
24030 Vercurago (Bg) Italy
Gadgets.

Comel S.r.l.
Via A Diaz 30/I
I-25100 Brescia, Italy
Electrical household appliances.

Cosatto SPA
P.O. Box 7-1-33035 Martignacco (UD) Italy

Keith Newmark Ltd.
Victoria Works, Institute Street
Padiham, Lancs BB12 8BB, England
Plastics for home and garden.

Odense
Woodenware Industry Ltd.
P.O.B. 39
DK-5240 Odense NO, Denmark
Revolving type rolling pins.

Euras GmbH
Robert-Bosch-Strass 11
D-8060 Dachau, West Germany
Small electrical appliances.

FRATELLI RE S.P.A.
S.S. 33 del Sempione 51
I-20017 RHO (Milano) Italy

Pudol Chemie, Gebr. Krumm KG
D-5241 Niederdreisbach, West Germany
Cleaning specialties.

SMAB S.r.l.
I-20050 Triuggo / MI, Italy
Scissors.

SOFTAN S.a.s.
9, Via G. Marconi
I-12040 Castelletto Stura CN - Italy
Chamois.

Haug Bursten
6 Foellstr.
D-8901 Koenigsbrunn, W. Germany
Scouring brushes and brooms.

FRANSPER di Francesca Speranza
2/15, Via i° Maggio
I-20068 Peschiera Borromeo (MI), Italy
Cleaning cloths, ironing board covers.

Eastern Counties Leather PLC
Sawston, Cambridge CB2 4EG, England
Chamois leather.

CADIA S.p.A.
25015 Desenzano Del Grada (Brescia) Italy
Heaters and radiators.

Salgotarjani Vasontode es Tuzhelygyar
P.O. Box 86, H-3101 Salgotarjan, Hungary
Iron foundry and stove factory.

Eastmead Electronics Ltd.
Eastmead Works, Lavant, Chester,
West Sussex, PO18 0DE, England
Electronic flying pest destroyer.

Dekur
P.O. Box 508
D-5400 Koblenz, West Germany
Insect repellers.

RITTO-Werk
Loh GmbH & Co. KG
c/o Mr. J. Hild, Exp. Mgr.
16 Industriestr.,
POB 110, D-6342 Haiger,
West Germany
Communications products.

Pragoexport
Advertising Dept.
34 Jungmannova
112 59 Praha 1, Czechoslovakia

Eckart-Werke
D-8510 Furth/Bayern
P.O. Box 101
Articles for Advent and Christmas
decorations, candles, Easter articles, festive
accessories.

Becker Antriebe GmbH
Postfach 67
D-6349 Sinn/Hessen, Germany
Tubular motors for shutters and awnings.

Chapter Thirteen

Untapped Taiwan Resources

Jong Diing Co. Ltd.
P.O. Box 16-527
Taipei, Taiwan
Hand painted silk wall fan and Chinese dolls.

Sunkist International Inc.
P.O. Box 39-617
Taipei, Taiwan
Key finder, colour changing mugs & porcelain wares.

Shin Chin Studio
P.O. Box 96-374
Taipei, Taiwan
Chinese oil painting.

Grand Idea Co. Ltd.
P.O. Box 58872
Taipei, Taiwan
Decorated fruit for Christmas decorations.

Long & High Enterprise Co. Ltd.
P.O. Box 447
Pan Chiao, Taiwan
Various cloisonne wares.

Formosa Merchandise Inc.
P.O. Box 101-56
Taipei, Taiwan
Giftware and Christmas decorative items.

Taiwan Longines Mfg. Co. Ltd.
P.O. Box 587
Taichung, Taiwan
Gifts and toys.

Huge-River Industry Corp.
P.O. Box 3-95
Taipei, Taiwan
Embroidered patch and customs emblem.

Peiwa Handicrafts Co. Ltd.
P.O. Bo 94-158
Taipei, Taiwan
Various handicrafts, ornaments, key chains,

Gaiety Co. Ltd.
P.O. Box 48-85
Taipei, Taiwan
Key finder, new feather handicraft and gifts.

Yestone Industrial Corp.
P.O. Box 87-479
Taipei, Taiwan
Gifts and handicrafts.

Wellsen Industrial Co. Ltd.
P.O. Box 11066
Taipei, Taiwan
Promotional items & gifts.

Grand Hill Services Co. Ltd.
P.O. Box 12-35
Peitou
Taipei, Taiwan, R.O.C.
Gifts and toys.

Chi Lung Union Works Co. Ltd.
P.O. Box 58907
Taipei, Taiwan
Three-dimensional picture with clock & wall plaque.

Ming I Industry Co. Ltd.
P.O. Box 39-1255
Taipei, Taiwan
Hanging decorations for Christmas with light.

Robert, Peter Associates Inc. Ltd.
P.O. Box 2-085
Pei Tou
Taipei, Taiwan, R.O.C.
Various styles porcelain wares & Christmas decoration.

Wan Yuan Trading Co. Ltd.
3/F., No. 74, Sec. 2
Chung King S. Road
Taipei, Taiwan, R.O.C.
Fashion key chain, brooches & gifts.

Chan Lian Handicraft Mfg. Co. Ltd.
P.O. Box 358 Pan Chiao
Taipei Hsien, Taiwan, R.O.C.
Chinese knot decorated mirror and screen,

Nork Huang Industrial Co. Ltd.
P.O. Box 26-935
Taipei, Taiwan
Fine earthenware and porcelainwares.

Cotter Enterprise Co. Ltd.
P.O. Box 92 Shalu
Taichung Hsien, Taiwan, R.O.C.
Wooden handicrafts.

Bestprofit Products Inc.
P.O. Box 30-590
Taipei, Taiwan
Porcelain ware, glassware & Christmas
decorations.

Full Luck Printing Co. Ltd.
P.O. Box 68-916
Taipei, Taiwan
Color separation services and color printing
gift boxes, greeting cards, publication &
catalogues.

Jewel Shine Industrial Corp.
P.O. Box 7-225
Taipei, Taiwan
Stationery organizer and gifts.

Spark Gold Co.
P.O. Box 37-76
Taipei, Taiwan
Ball point pen, mechanical pencil & rolling
pen, etc.

Dolly's International Corp.
P.O. Box 68-378
Taipei, Taiwan
Stationery products.

John's Union Enterprise Co. Ltd.
P.O. Box 68-462
Taipei, Taiwan
Photo album.

Super Lines International Corp.
P.O. Box 81-722
Taipei, Taiwan
Gold plated book mark for promoting gifts.

Paishih Stationery Industry Co. Ltd.
P.O. Box 59014
Taipei, Taiwan
Ball point pens.

Fulin Graphic Arts Inc.
P.O. Box 28-35
Taipei, Taiwan
CM photo originals are demanded offer,
exchange, agency, for rent and any beauties
for calendar, poster, catalogue originals
(slide).

Sun Ho Merchandise Co. Ltd.
P.O. Box 24-539
Taipei, Taiwan
Various styles dolls.

Dominion Equipment & Service Corp.
P.O. Box 82-71
Taipei, Taiwan
All golf equipments.

Win On Enterprise Inc.
P.OO. Box 68-354
Taipei, Taiwan
Inflatable toys.

K-Moebel Co. Ltd.
2/F., No. 43, Nung-An Street
Taipei, Taiwan, R.O.C.
Watersport equipment & physical exercise
support.

Norstar International Co. Ltd.
P.O. Box 46-362
Taipei, Taiwan
Baseball caps and PVC sporting caps.

Puzzleworks Corp.
P.O. Box 373
Kaohsiung, Taiwan
Educational preschool toys and jigsaw
puzzles.

Columbus Mfg. Corp.
6/F., China Daily News Building, 131
Sung Chaing Road
Taipei, Taiwan
Eyeglasses for diving.

Golden Shine Inc.
3/F., No. 152, Ankung Road, Nei-Hu
Taipei, Taiwan, R.O.C.
Tennis racquets.

Aurora Board Industrial Co. Ltd.
P.O. Box 131
Kaohsiung, Taiwan
Wind Surfer sailing board.

Carson Trading Co.
P.O. Box 18-21
Taipei, Taiwan
Golf equipment & tennis accessories.

Ideation Industry Co. Ltd.
P.O. Box 406
Taipei, Taiwan
BMX bikes & bicycles.

ASO Enterprise Co. Ltd.
P.O. Box 593
Taipei, Taiwan
Genuine leather handbags & travel bags.

Lougei S.A.
P.O. Box 7-478
Taipei, Taiwan
Sporting shoes.

Royal Ace Enterprise Co. Ltd.
P.O. Box 26-643
Taipei, Taiwan
Snake skin belts & leather garments.

Lung Dragon Industry Co. Ltd.
P.O. Box 68-535
Taipei, Taiwan
Sporting footwears.

Lakewood Enterprises Ltd.
P.O. Box 22303
Taipei, Taiwan
Baby shoes and sporting footwear.

Join Product Co. Ltd.
P.O. Box 68-1590
Taipei, Taiwan
Footwear.

San Fui International Co.
P.O. Box 447
Tainan, Taiwan
Children's garments and frock-coat.

Free Bird Enterprise Co. Ltd.
P.O. Box 12185
Taipei, Taiwan
Fashion footwear.

Z & Z Far East Corp.
P.OO. Box 96-244
Taipei, Taiwan
Table cloth, napkin and PE laundry bags.

Lefrong Enterprise Co. Ltd.
P.O. Box 59151
Taipei, Taiwan
Fashion ladies handbags.

Winbest Co. Ltd.
P.O. Box 24-672
Taipei, Taiwan
Sporting bags and traveling bags.

Hoo Tai Enterprises Inc.
P.O. Box 67-502
Taipei, Taiwan
Wetsuits, gloves, boots & water ski
accessories.

Golden Line Business Corp.
P.O. Box 1876
Kaohsiung, Taiwan
PP woven sacks & PE woven sacks.

G-Line Plastic Industrial Corp.
P.O. Box 7-557
Taipei, Taiwan
PVC vinyl floor tiles.

Shin Shyu Enterprise Co. Ltd.
P.O. Box 53-1194
Taipei, Taiwan
Locks.

Moi Hua Industries Co. Ltd.
14, Lane 332, Cheng Kuo Road
Ping Tung, Taiwan, R.O.C.
Lauan solid timber doors.

Dynamic Co. Ltd.
P.O. Box 3164
Taipei, Taiwan
Scissors.

United Relience Enterprise Ltd.
8F-5, 201, Ho Ping East Road, Section 2
Taipei, Taiwan, R.O.C.
Hardware, building material and machine
tools.

Siang & Siu Co. Ltd.
P.O. Box 7-130
Taipei, Taiwan
Mini electric sewing machine.

Shenq Horng Enterprise Co. Ltd.
P.O. Box 3861
Taipei, Taiwan
Genuine jewelry & imitation jewelry.

Hong Mei Coral Jewelry Factory
Exporter & Wholesale
19, Lane 226, Sung Chiang Road
Taipei, Taiwan, R.O.C.
All fashion jewelry.

Mario King Enterprise Co. Ltd.
121, Section 3, Nanking East Road
Taipei, Taiwan, R.O.C.
Fashion jewelry.

Sailing International Co. Ltd.
P.O. Box 22497
Taipei, Taiwan
Fahsion imitation jewelry.

Chang Hai Crafts Co. Ltd.
P.O. Box 68-701
Taipei, Taiwan
Semi-precious stone, rings & necklaces.

Do-Well Enterprises Inc.
P.O. Box 35-125
Taichung, Taiwan
Pouches for jewelry, smoke pipe, cosmetics,
souvenirs.

Pro-Worlds Corp.
P.O. Box 73-200
Taipei, Taiwan
Imitation jewelry.

Ronnie International Ltd.
9-1 Fl, Yang Te Building, No. 127
Kee Lung Road, Section 1
Taipei, Taiwan
Artificial flowers.

Channel Co. Ltd.
P.O. Box 55-612
Taipei, Taiwan
Semi-precious stone & coral jewelry.

River Enterprise Co. Ltd.
P.O. Box 22123
Taipei, Taiwan
Natural Fasion jewelry.

One Dash Industrial Co. Ltd.
P.O. Box 94-142
Taipei, Taiwan
Imitation jewelry & beads.

Ay Shu Enterprise Co. Ltd.
P.O. Box 21-80
Taipei, Taiwan
Fashion jewelry & synthetic gems in 925, 14K.

Peng Chia Enterprise Co. Ltd.
P.O. Box 87-412
Taipei, Taiwan
MOP & lapis necklaces & shell jewelry.

Dosway Merchandise Corp.
P.O. Box 55-1351
Taipei, Taiwan
Beautiful & fashion jewelry.

Exartech International Corp.
P.O. Box 37-11
Taipei, Taiwan
Hair ornaments & necklaces.

New Star Corporation
P.O. Box 68-1799
Taipei, Taiwan
Taiwan jade & paua shell.

Bettyjou Industrial Co. Ltd.
P.O. Box 39-790
Taipei, Taiwan
Jewelry & decoration.

Joe Kang Manufacturers International Corp
P.O. Box 46-490
Taipei, Taiwan
Imitation necklace, rings, brooches & hair ornaments.

Great Pluto Industrial Corp.
P.O. Box 84-126
Taipei, Taiwan
Fine jewelry & natural color stones.

Best Control Industrial Co. Ltd.
P.O. Box 2-205 Pei Tou
Taipei, Taiwan, R.O.C.
Newest style sunglasses, reading glass & spectacle frames.

Bridgehead Industrial Co. Ltd.
P.O. Box 70-358
Taipei, Taiwan
Cloisonne jewelry.

Taiwan Fu Cheng Enterprise Inc.
P.O. Box 83-79
Taipei, Taiwan
Hair ornaments & jewelry.

Pan Formosa Art Co. Ltd.
P.O. Box 68-1625
Taipei, Taiwan
Costume jewelry & fashion hair ornaments.

Chu Sheng Industrial Co. Ltd.
P.O. Box 30-545
Taipei, Taiwan
Moslem bead & necklace.

Long Kuan Industrial Co.
P.O. Box 48-4
Taipei, Taiwan
Custom jewelry.

Baobab Tree Co. Ltd.
3/F., No. 88, Section 2
Tung Hua Street
Taipei, Taiwan, R.O.C.
Miracle can opener & shrinky magic card.

Starfield Corp.
P.O. Box 68-2242
Taipei, Taiwan
Tooth brushes.

Cavalier Industrial Co. Ltd.
P.O. Box 84-823
Taipei, Taiwan
Hi-intensive flexi light tool.

Chapter Fourteen

Untapped Hong Kong Resources

Tseyu International Trading Co. Ltd.
20 Bedford Road, Casey Industrial Building
2/F., Taikoktsui
Kowloon, Hong Kong
Sewing kits, industrial & domestic threads,
high quality spun polyester sewing threads.

Universal Belts Wholesale Company
223A Tai Nam Street, G/F.
(near Nam Cheong Street), Shamshuipo
Kowloon, Hong Kong
Belts in leather, imitation leather, canvas,
PVC coated cotton, metals.

Wai Wing Metal Manufactory Ltd.
52, Yu Chau Street, G/F.
Shamshuipo
Kowloon, Hong Kong
Metal accessories for garments, shoes, toys,
handbags & luggage, high quality belt
buckles.

Winner International
Office A, 1/F., Tai Cheong Mansion
36-38 Nam Cheong Street
Kowloon, Hong Kong
Clothing accessories, high quality knitted
gloves, scarves, hats, belts.

Winner International
Office A, 1/F., Tai Cheong Mansion
36-38 Nam Cheong Street
Kowloon, Hong Kong
Clothing accessories, high quality knitted
gloves, scarves, hats, belts.

Wing Lee P.V.C. Leather Factory
Flat H, Blk. A, 3/F.
Marvel Industrial Building
25-31 Kwai Fung Road
Kwai Chung, N.T., Hong Kong
Mens' fashionable nylon knitted with PVC
combination of PVC belts with fancy metal
buckles.

Yau Luen Necktie Fty.
21A Ming Wah Industrial Building
17-33 Wang Lung Street
Tsuen Wan, N.T., Hong Kong
Badges for promotional purposes,
customers' logos, trademarks or slogans
woven or embroidered in fine detail, borders
well-trimmed with over-locking.

Bo-Bo Manufacturing Company
Luen Hing Industrial Building, Mezz Floor
86 Tai Kok Tsui Road
Kowloon, Hong Kong
Babies' bibs, aprons & trainer pants in
cotton, PVC, gingham, terry &
polyester/cotton knitted.

Carson Manufactory
Wai Yick Industrial Building
7/F., 46-48 Anchor Street
Tai Kok Tsui
Kowloon, Hong Kong
Fashionable ladies' panties, babies' &
children's wear, weekly briefs, tanga briefs
in cotton/nylon/synethtic.

Chang & Company
2101, Hop Fat Commercial Centre
490-492 Nathan Road
Kowloon, Hong Kong
Men's, ladies' & children's underwear,
including vest/brief sets) made of cotton,
nylon & other CVC & CVS materials.

Carson Manufactory
Wai Yick Industrial Building
7/F., 46-48 Anchor Street
Tai Kok Tsui
Kowloon, Hong Kong
Ladies' panties, babies' & children's wear,
weekly briefs, tanga briefs in
cotton/nylon/synthetic materials.

Chun Wan Garment Factory
Flats A/C, 25/F., Blk. 2
Golden Dragan Industrial Centre
162-170 Tai Lin Pai Road
Kwai Chung, N.T., Hong Kong
Anoraks, parkas & ski-jackets for men,
women & children.

Ever Good Garment Fty.
Flat 4, 12/F., Wealthy Industrial Building
22-26 Wing Yip Street
Kwai Chung, N.T., Hong Kong
Babies' cotton knitted printed bibs, aprons,
diapers, pyjamas, T-shirts & ladies' printed
nightgowns.

Fasontex Sportswear Fashion Ltd.
13B, Tomson Commercial Building
8 Thomson Road
Wanchai, Hong Kong
Coveralls in rubberized oxford nylon quality
with all seams taped, guaranteed 100%
waterproof, T/C protective coveralls with
quilted padding inside.

Galaton Co. Ltd.
P.O. Box 71562, Kowloon Central Post
Office
Kowloon, Hong Kong
Polyester/cotton fishing vests &
ramie/cotton hunting suits.

Chak Fun Company Limited
5/F., Flat C, Selwyn Factory Building
404 Kwun Tong Road
Kwun Tong, Kowloon, Hong Kong
LCD products, simple module to advanced
scientific calculator.

Bota International, Inc.
7/F., Goodfit Comm. Building
7 Fleming Road
Hong Kong
Wall/table ceramic clocks, calendars &
novelties, advertising premiums,
promotional gifts. Company names and
logos, custom designs.

Dragon Light Watch, Ltd.
Room 1707, Good Hope Building
612-618 Nathan Road
Kowloon, Hong Kong
Quartz analog & mechanical watches fashion
& novelty, rolling & moving objects.

East Asia Watch Co. Ltd.
The Comercial Bank of Hong Kong
Building
15/F., 120-126 Des Voeux Road, Central
Hong Kong
Analog quartz & mechanical watches.

Hwa's Trading Co.
Room 1008 Arion Commercial Centre
2-12 Queen's Road, West
Hong Kong
Analog & mechanical watches, national flags
& laser dials. HA-08 series with see through
& 3ATM water-resistance.

Genuine Consultants
2203M, Nan Fung Centre
22/F., 298 Castle Peak Road
Tsuen Wan, N.T., Hong Kong
Wall/table clocks, wood or lacquer finish,
hand-painted.

Isis Electronics
19B Shiu Fung Commercial Building
51-53 Johnston Road
Wanchai, Hong Kong
Electronic & miscellaneous products,
promotional and advertising items.

HK Watchbands Corp.
88 Nathan Road, 2/F., A
Kowloon, Hong Kong
Metal watchbands.

Jean Pierre Product (Far East) Co.
"D1", 14/F., Mirador Mansion
54-64 Nathan Road
Tsimshatsui, Kowloon, Hong Kong
Analog quartz watches & LCD watches.

KH Watchbands Corp.
88 Nathan Road, 2/F., A
Kowloon, Hong Kong
Leather watchbands.

Lee Shing Metal Mfg.
Flat A & B, 12/F.
Wai Yick Industrial Building, 99 Bedford
Road
Taikoktsui, Kowloon, Hong Kong
Metal watch bands.

Milan Co.
Room 1205, Bank Centre, 636 Nathan Road
Kowloon, Hong Kong
Watch bands.

Sharp Fly Company Ltd.
Texaco Road, Industrial Centre
Flat A3, 10/F.
256-264 Texaco Road
Tsuen Wan, N.T., Hong Kong
Nylon, PVC watch bands.

Oversea Nation Limited
604 Wong House
26-30 Des Voeux Road, West
Hong Kong
Analog & mechanical watches.

Shui Run Industrial Ltd.
Flat D & E, 13/F.
Mai On Industrial Building
No. 17-21 Kung Yip Street
Kwai Chung, N.T., Hong Kong
Stainless steel watch bands & bracelets.

Tai Tung Watch Manufactory Ltd.
Room 606, Fife Building
699 Nathan Road, Mongkok
Kowloon, Hong Kong
LCD quartz watches, pen watches.

Trustworthy Industries Ltd.
603, Tung Wah Mansion
203 Hennessy Road
Hong Kong
Analog quartz watches & LCD watches.

Trans-Tronic Manufacturing Ltd.
120 Chiap Thong Building
321 Tokwawan Road
Kowloon, Hong Kong
Quartz watches & clocks.

Universal Manufacturer
18/F., Wing Fat Commercial Building
216-218 Aberdeen Main Road
Hong Kong
LCD watches, pendant watches & gift sets,
calculator watches, LCD watches &
modules.

Venson Watch Co.
Room 1202, 12/F.
Java Commercial Centre, 128 Java Road
North Point, Hong Kong
Analog quartz & LCD watches.

Wai Keung Metal Manufactory Ltd.
14/F., Blk. G, Phase 2
Kongsway Industrial Building,
173-175 Wo Yi Hop Road
Kwai Chung, N.T., Hong Hong
Watchcases, watch bands.

Wing Hang Watch Co.
Room 1802 Tai Shing Commercial Building
498-500 Nathan Road
Yaumati, Kowloon, Hong Kong
Analog quartz, LCD watches, roskopf &
lever watches fitted with Swiss, French,
German & Russian movements. Pendants,
rings pocket-size, convertibles, bracelet
watches.

Wing Yip Industrial Co.
2ABC, 2/F., Blk. 4
San Po Kong Fty. Building
Kowloon, Hong Kong
LCD watches, display watches & thin pocket
calculator.

Au's The Long Life Plastic & Metal Mfg.
Ltd.
3/F., Eastern Industrial Building
42-50 Kwai Ting Road
Kwai Chung, N.T., Hong Kong
Plastic items, combs & brushes, stationery,
toys, household items, buttons & buckles,
beads, polymotif sheets, handbags &
handles, clips, kid's toilet seats, plastic
framed mirrors, flower pots, baskets &
other horticultural items.

Adwell Corporation
706 Li Po Chun Chambers
185-195 Des Voeux Road, Central
Hong Kong
Advertising materials, jackets, anoraks,
caps, hats, umbrellas, shopping & travelling
bags, stationery.

Capital Embroidering & Weaving Ltd.
Flat B, 23/F., Ming Wah Industrial Building
17-33 Wang Lung Street
Tsuen Wan, N.T., Hong Kong
Woven & embroidered badges, club-ties.

First Plastic Factory
Blk. A, 5/F., On Fat Industrial Building
12-18 Kwai Wing Road
Kwai Chung, N.T., Hong Kong
Plastic hairbrushes.

The Fair Corporation
Room 1228, Star House
Tsimshatsui
Kowloon, Hong Kong
Fashion accessories.

Golden Industrial Co. (Golden Enterprise)
UUnit 10, 2/F., Phase II,
Newport Centre, 116 Ma Tau Kok Road
Kowloon, Hong Kong
Halloween wigs, afro plaits, curly plaits,
afro wigs, doll's wigs & stuffed doll's.

Grand Metal Works Ltd.
1 Walnut Street, 9/F.
Kowloon, Hong Kong
Snap buttons, rivets, trouser hooks, eyelets,
jingle bells, battery caps, buckles.

Hong Tat Cap & Hat Manufactory
Enterprise
Co. Ltd.
6/F., Flat 'T, U & O', Blk. 2
Kinho Industrial Building
14-24 Au Pui Wan Street
Fotan, Shatin, N.T., Hong Kong
Baseball caps, mainly to U.S.A.

Hong Tat Cap & Hat Manufactory
Enterprise
Co. Ltd.
6/F., Flat 'T, U & O', Blk. 2
Kinho Industrial Building
14-24 Au Pui Wan Street
Fotan, Shatin, N.T., Hong Kong
Caps and hats.

Jacky Knitting & Trading Co. Ltd.
Flat A & D, 3/F.
Fu Hop Factory Building
209-211 Wai Yip Street
Kwun Tong
Kowloon, Hong Kong
Knitted gloves, hats & scarves, lambswool,
acrylic & wool.

Interhats Manufacturing Limited
6/F., Aberdeen Industrial Building
236 Aberdeen Main Road
Hong Kong
Fashion hats & caps, sports caps & tennis
visors.

Jeanswear Sewing Accessories Co. Ltd.
16-18 Wah Sing Street
22/F., Blk. D, Bold Win Industrial Building
Kowloon, Hong Kong
Polyester & cotton sewing thread & kits,
accessories.

Capital Shoes Fty. Ltd.
29 Hing Yip Street, 1/F., Timely Fty.
Building
Kwun Tong
Kowloon, Hong Kong
Children's fashionable sandals & shoes.

Chi Shing Industrial Factory
Flat H, 5/F., Kim Tak Building
328 Nathan Road
Kowloon, Hong Kong
Beaded & embroidery products, purses,
earrings, bracelets, handbags & glass cases &
other beaded trimmings, motifs.

Cheung Sing Metal Manufactory
Flat 18A, 10/F., Profit Industrial Building
1-15 Kwai Fung Crescent
Kwai Chung, N.T., Hong Kong
Garment accessories for clothes, handbags.
Tie-pins, buttons & old brass enamelled top
snap buttons, buckles.

Chong Fai Belt Factory
No. 1, 6/F., Wah Luen Industrial Building
15-21 Wong Chuk Yeung Street
Fo Tan, Shatin, N.T., Hong Kong
Ladies' & mens' belts & handbags, leather &
various materials, fashionable & classical
styles, elaborate design & workmanship.

Chung Fung Trading Company
Room 607, 6/F.
Universal Commercial Building
69 Peking Road, Tsimshatsui
Kowloon, Hong Kong
Ladies stylish belts in leather & a variety of
other materials.

CNL Company
Flat B, 3/F., Room 6
Wah Kai Industrial Centre
221 Texaco Road
Tsuen Wan, N.T., Hong Kong
Hats, caps & customer-designed, woven &
embroidered badges.

Chung Yun Ties Co.
9 Reclamation Street, 2/F.
Kowloon, Hong Kong
Weaving, embroidery, silk linings, men's
neckties including leather.

D.S.C. Direct Sales Co. Ltd.
Unit 502, Houston Centre, 63 Mody Road
Tsimshatsui East
Kowloon, Hong Kong
Belts, customers' own patterns & designs.

Evergreen Products Fty.
Block B, 7/F., Mai Luen Industrial Building
No. 23-31 Kung Yip Street
Kwai Chung, N.T., Hong Kong
Human hair & synthetic, men's & ladies'
mannequin heads, children's, doll wigs, afro
wigs, hair pieces & braids, carnival-colored
wigs & window display wigs, Santa Claus &
judges wigs, halloween disguise products &
clown supplies, all beauty accessories.

Kai Lai Metal & Plastic Ornaments Fty.
2 Tai Yau Street, Flat D & E, 10/F.
Wong King Industrial Building
Sanpokong
Kowloon, Hong Kong
"Make-your-own necklaces" sets, friction
toys & powerful spring mechanism toys, hair
ornaments & imitation jewelry.

Lee Brothers Hats Fty, Ltd.
Blk. B, 12/F., Mon Hing Fty. Building
20 Catchick Street
Hong Kong
Hats & caps for advertising, sport-caps &
fashion hats.

Long Best Development Ltd.
5/F., Flat C, Selwyn Factory Building
404 Kwun Tong Road
Kwun Tong
Kowloon, Hong Kong
Children's fashionable shoes.

Luen Fat Chemical Production Co. Ltd.
Flat A & C, 1/F., Blk. 9
Thian's Industrial Centre, Lot 74
Hung Cheung Road
Tuen Mun, N.T., Hong Kong
EVA, PVC & rubber, sandals & foaming
sheets, plastic straps, buyers' designed soles.

Mascot Hair Accessories Co. Ltd.
902, Manning House
38-48 Queen's Road, Central
Hong Kong
Hair ornaments, plastic & metal, hair slides
& clips, headbands, ponytail holders, hair
combs, plastic brushes.

M.G.B. Industrial Co. Ltd.
613 Tung Ying Building
100 Nathan Road
Kowloon, Hong Kong
PVC raincoats.

Modern Industries
87 Third Street, G/F.
Hong Kong
Advertising caps, bobs & visors.

Ming Ming Industrial Co.
Room 1701, Beverley Commercial Centre
87-105 Chatham Road
Kowloon, Hong Kong
Nylon fiber gloves, cotton crochet gloves,
angora gloves.

Oriental Thread Co. Ltd.
Flat E, 18/F.
Superluck Industrial Centre, Phase 2
57 Sha Tsui Road
Tsuen Wan, N.T., Hong Kong
Sewing kits, customers' name, logo &
advertisements printed on covering case.

Pak Tak Leather Wae Fty. Ltd.
Flat C & D, 3/F., Blk. 1
Kwai Tak Industrial Centre
15-33 Kwai Tak Street
Kwai Chung, N.T., Hong Kong
Belts, leather, imitation leather, PVC, cotton
fashionable belts.

San Kay Industrial Limited
Blk. G, 12/F., Kwai Shing Industrial
Building
42-46 Tai Lin Pai Road
Kwai Chung, N.T., Hong Kong
Knitted gloves, mittens, hats, legwarmers &
scarves, fancy & jacquard patterns. 100%
acrylic or wool, mixtures, lambswool,
angora, for men, ladies, girls & infants,
babies.

Sun Ray Manufactory
151-7 Wo Yi Hop Road, 3/F.
Victory Industrial Building
Kwai Chung, N.T., Hong Kong
Ladies' & mens' belts of genuine leather &
various kinds of material, fashionable &
classical styles, elaborate design and
workmanship.

Tack Cheung Fat Co. Ltd.
1703 Alliance Building
130 Connaught Road, C.
Hong Kong
Beach sandals & elastic bands made of PP,
cotton, nylon yarn & polyester.

Suun Wah Weaving & Tie Fty.
65-67 Chai Wan Kok Street, 3/F.
Tsuen Wan, N.T., Hong Kong
Embroidered badges, jacquard polyester
fabrics for ties, scarves & silk linings,
schoolties, club-ties & badges.

Tak Lee Company
Flat A, 8/F., Sing Kui Commercial Building
27 Des Voeux Road, West
Hong Kong
Rubber products, household & industrial
gloves, boots, sandals, rubber bands,
balloons, bicycle tires.

Tany Trading Company
P.O. Box 33663, Sheung Wan Post Office
Hong Kong
Accu-massage sandals & MaganeFlux belts.

Tat Shing Metal Mfy.
206, Lai Chi Kok Road, G/F.
Shamshuipo
Kowloon, Hong Kong
Gold-plated & silver-plated metal buckles,
locks, frames, oranaments for belts,
handbags, shoes & luggage.

Tin Shun Hong
Blk. B, 18/F., Cheung Ka Industrial
Building
345 Des Voeux Road, West
Hong Kong
All sorts of shoes, custom-made orders.

Melleyloy Tape Mfy. Co. Ltd.
13/F., Blk. A & C
King Yip Fty. Building, 59 King Yip Street
Kwun Tong
Kowloon, Hong Kong
Video cassettes (VHS), video tapes, VO &
parts.

Kun Ka Engeneering Co. Ltd.
Room 1405-8 Hing Yip Commercial Centre
272-284 Des Voeux Road, Central
Hong Kong
Stereo radio cassetes, radios, power supplies,
night lights, quartz clocks, antennas, walkie
talkies.

P & F Products Ltd.
9/F., Block F, Selwyn Factory Building
404 Kwun Tong Road, Kwun Tong
Kowloon, Hong Kong
Electronic telephones, telephone accessories,
LED clocks, alarm clocks.

Primatronix Ltd.
IUnit 11, 10/F., Wing Hang Industrial
Building
13-29 Kwai Hei Street
Kwai Chung, N.T., Hong Kong
Electronic products specializing in telephone
& answering machines, calculators.

Safrex Electronic Co. Ltd.
8/F., Siu Ying Commercial Building
151-155 Queen's Road, C.
Hong Kong
Emergency alarm for personal protection.

Usance Company Ltd.
V. Heun Building, 11/F.
138 Queen's Road, Central
Hong Kong
Radios, model 710,6 transistors + 2 diodes,
2-band MW/SW, operated by UM 1×3
batteries or 110 volt AC, w/case.

Golden Dragon Rattan Ware Co. Ltd.
7-11 Kimberley Street, On Luen Building
4/F., Blk. B & D
Kowloon, Hong Kong
Rattan furniture & basketware.

Grand Union Trading Co. Ltd.
Sun House, 7/F.
181 Des Voeux Road, Central
Hong Kong
Household enamelware & cookware.

Hai Feng Wicker Products Ltd.
11/F., Flat A, Hyfco Industrial Building
Blk. III, Fuk Lee Street
Kowloon, Hong Kong
Wicker ware, trunks, hampers, baskets,
planters, trays, vases, plate holders, full
range painted w/handcrafted pattern.

Yu's Million Electronics Co. Ltd.
17 Cheung Lee Street, 8/F.
Chi Ko Industrial Building
Chai Wan, Hong Hong
Battery chargers, adaptors, power-supplies,
rechargeable drills & all kinds of audio
cables.

Bernard Hong Kong Company
1101 Mongkok Commercial Centre
16 Argyle Street
Kowloon, Hong Kong
Am/FM stereo radio cassette player with 2
fold back/detachable speakers, accessories.

Allitex Electronics Mfg. Co.
P.O. Box 70
Tsuen Wan, N.T., Hong Kong
Torch radios MW/FM/LW, MW/SW 2
bands, 3 bands, 4 bands & auto electrical
warning appliances.

Aloha Industrial Company
Flat F., Stage 1, 22/F.
Tung Chun Industrial Building
9-11 Cheung Wing Road
Kwai Chung, N.T., Hong Kong
Battery operated novel electronic items, such
as visor cap radios, mini size FM band
radios, bathroom radio & telephone.

Blue Light Trading (HK) Co.
Beverley Commercial Centre, Room 1111,
11/F.
87-105 Chatham Road, Tsimshatsui
Kowloon, Hong Hong
Various kinds of radios, AM/FM Mono
Headphone Radio, Stereo Slim Radio with
Clip, Portable Radio.

Freeair Electronics Limited
A1 Tung Wong House, 2/F.
18 Main Street, East
Shaukiwan, Hong Kong
"Freeair" brand two band radio with
flashlight, two band radio with flashlight &
blinking light, one band bicycle radio with
sportlight & alarm, one band radio with
mini torch & music box & door chimes.

Faithful Trading Center
Room 804, 804A, 811A, Wu Sang House
655 Nathan Road
Kowloon, Hong Kong
Electronic key pager, locates keys.

Fujicom Denshi (HK) Company
Unit No. 2, 8/F., Profit Industrial Building
1-15 Kwai Fung Crescent
Kwai Chung, N.T., Hong Kong
Video cassettes, video alarm, V-O cassette &
loading equipment supply & head cleaners.

Hang Fai Industrial Co.
Blk. H, 2/F., Win Field Industrial Building
3 Kin Kwan Street
Tuen Mun, N.T., Hong Kong
Plastic & metal household wares.

Highway Enterprises Ltd.
Unit 5, 1/F., Kinglet Industrial Building
21-23 Shing Wan Road, Tai Wai
Shatin, N.T., Hong Kong
Chrome-plated & silver plated tableware &
household articles.

Hong Kong Porcelain & Copper Wares Fty.
11/F., Flat A, HYFCO Industrial Building
Blk. III, Fuk Lee Street, Tai Kok Tsui
Kowloon, Hong Kong
Solid brass giftware, banks, planters, tea-
caddies, trays, oil lamps, candlesticks, vases,
trivets, stationeries.

Johnson Measures & Weights Ltd.
Flat C & D, 7/F., Yip Fat Fty. Building
77 Hoi Yuen Road, Kwun Tong
Kowloon, Hong Kong
Household utensils, scales & all kinds of
steel tape measures.

Ken Yau Metal Works
Flat M, 16/F., Vigor Industrial Building
Ta Chuen Ping Street
K.C.T.L. No. 302
Kwai Chung, N.T., Hong Kong
Multi-purpose bottle & can openers &
kitchenwares, metal gift & premium items.

Koon Wah Metal Mfg. Fty.
Bold Win Industrial Building, Blk. C, 1/F.
16-18 Wah Sing Street
Kwai Chung, N.T., Hong Kong
Plastic & metal water sprayers & houseware
merchandise.

Kowloon Chemicals Industrial Co. Ltd.
20 Wing Hong Street, 4/F.
Kowloon, Hong Kong
Melamine ware, tea sets, table-ware &
ashtrays, bakelite accessories for metal
cookware.

Lee Sang (Chuen Kee) Manufacturing Fty.
Ltd.
Blk. A, 11/F., Yee Lim Industrial Building
Stage III, 6-8 Kin Chuen Street
Kwai Chung, N.T., Hong Kong
"Flexi-String" space-saver for bathroom's
appliance or Christmas cards.

Max International Corp.
G.P.O. Box 6748
Hong Kong
Chrome/silver-plated trays, kitchenware,
household goods.

Pui Hing Metal Ware Factory
Stage 1, Tung Chun Industrial Building
11/F., Blk. A, 9-11 Cheung Wing Road
Kwai Chung, N.T., Hong King
Householdware & kitchenware.

Well Leader Industrial Co.
Blk. A8, 11/F., Delya Industrial Centre
TMTL 164 Shek Pai Tau Road
Tuen Mun, N.T., Hong Kong
Plastic kitchenware & household items.

Wellstand Company Ltd.
Room 514, Hunghom Commercial Centre
Tower B, 37 Ma Tau Wai Road
Kowloon, Hong Kong
Kitchenware & gift items.

Wing Kwong Industrial Co. Ltd.
Room 127-129, 1/F., blk. 1
Tai Wo Hau Government Fty. Building
Sha Tsui Road
Tsuen Wan, N.T., Hong Kong
Silver-plated, brass-plated, chrome-plated
giftware & tableware.

Wood Lick Plastic Company
Mon Hing Factory Building, 7/F., 'B'
20 Catchick Street
Kennedy Town, Hong Kong
Plastic disposable cutlery & fancy plastic
cocktail sticks with customers' special
design.

Yewell Products Co.
Flat P, Q, R, Mezz./F., Wai Lee Building
997 King's road
Quarry Bay, Hong Kong
Nylon/P.E. food covers, PVC vinyl/cotton
aprons, pot holders & various kinds
household articles.

Yu Lung Trading Co.
701 Blissful Building
243-247 Des Voeux Road, Central
Hong Kong
Cushion covers, square & round shaped,
gold & silver thread embroidered, designs
with typical oriental motifs.

Alain Chan & Associates
21 Lock Road, 3/F.
Kowloon, Hong Kong
Free size, standard size & carved opals in all
sizes & shapes.

Anthony Company
Room 701, Chatham Commercial Centre
45-51 Chatham Road
Tsimshatsui South
Kowloon, Hong Kong
Semi-precious stones & clasps, lapis lazuli,
turquoise, coral, amethyst, tourmaline, jade,
in beads, cabochons.

Artland Plastic — Jewellery Factory
B1, 13/F., Mei Hing Industrial Building
16-18 Hing Yip Street
Ksun Tong
Kowloon, Hong Kong
Fas

Sin Ching Kee
11 Man On Street, G/F.
Kowloon, Hong Kong
Wooden plate & vase stands.

Sun Ling & Company
12/F., Cheung Wei Industrial Building
42 Lee Chung Street
Chaiwan, Hong Kong
Plastic products, water jugs & cups to picnic
sets.

Sun Tien Brushes Co.
10 Wing Hong Street
China Pacific Industrial Building, 7/F.
Castle Peak Road
Kowloon, Hong Kong
Household brushes, tooth brushes, paint
brushes, paint rollers, clothing brushes, hair
brushes, nail brushes, shaving brushes,
cleaning brushes, industrial brushes &
brushes for all construction uses &
handtools.

Sunlight Manufactory
Blk. B, 5/F., Gold Sun Industry Building
No. 23 Tin Hau Road
Tuen Mun, N.t., Hong Kong
Plastic hangers for hanging towels, light
dresses, small utensils & tiny tools.

Tai Fat Manufacturing Company
Room 1945-6, Chun Shing Factory Estate
Kwai Fuk Road
Kwai Chung, Hong Kong
Wooden & bamboo toothpicks,
party/cocktail picks & parasols, traditional
Chinese decorative picks, barbecue picks &
straws.

Tai Hing Metal Manufactory
12/F., Blk. K & 10/F., Blk. A
Wah Fung Industrial Building, Stage 2
Hing Fong Road
Ha Kwai Chung, N.T., Hong Kong

Wah Foo Trade Co
(Welcome Plastic & Metal Mfy.)
Room 2210, Tsuen Wan Industrial Centre
220-248 Texaco Road
Tsuen Wan, N.T., Hong Kong
Vacuum flasks & enamelware.

Wah Tat Plastic Works Ltd.
12-18 Kwai Wing Road
On Fat Industrial Building, 3/F.
Kwai Chung, Hong Kong
Plastic combs, hair brushes, plastic cups,
plates, baskets & photo-frames, cosmetic
mirrors.

Wah Tung China Co.
Cat Street Galleries, 38 Lok Ku Road
Queen's Road, Central
Hong Kong
Antique porcelain reproduction.

Wang Tat Bakelite Fty. Ltd.
714 Prince Edward Road, 2/F.
San Po Kong
Kowloon, Hong Kong
Melamineware & no-porcelain products.

Way On Company
Room 405, Fife Building
699 Nathan Road
Kowloon, Hong Kong
Rattan furniture & baskets.

Man Wah Handicraft
32-34 Hong Keung Street, B3, 1/F.
San Po Kong
Kowloon, Hong Kong
Rayon brocade products, jewelery cases,
wallets, handbags, purses, cosmetic bags, eye
glasses bags, novelties & sundry items.

MST Productions Co. Ltd.
Bonsun Industrial Building, 8/F.
364-366 Sha Tsui Road
Tsuen Wan, N.T., Hong Kong
High quality ladies' fashionable handbags.

Ming Sze Handbag Mfg. Co.
7/F., Stage 2, Yip Fat Building
73-75 Hoi Yuen Road, Kwun Tong
Kowloon, Hong Kong
Fashionable hand-made genuine snake-skin
handbags, rhinestone evening bags, beaded
bags & purses of superb craftsmanship.

Neke Manufacturing Co.
Room 319, Beverley Commercial Centre,
3/F.
87-105 Chatham Road
Kowloon, Hong Kong
Handbags from evening to casual.

Sea Star Bags Manufactory Ltd.
1207-8 Tsuen Wan Industrial Centre
220-248 Texaco Road
Tsuen Wan, N.T., Hong Kong
High quality nylon PU & canvas extending
travelling bags, other travelling bags,
handbags & school bags.

Seasonal Bags
A4, 6/F., Yip Fung Industrial Building
28 Kwai Fung Crescent
Kwai Chung, N.T., Hong Kong
Handbags, wallets, key holders, in genuine
cow nappa & soft garment leather.

Shing Fat Handbag Fty.
Blk. B2, 5/F., Hong Kong Industrial Centre
489-491 Castle Peak Road
Kowloon, Hong Kong
Foldable bags for travelling, sporting,
shopping in PVC, PU, nylon, oxford &
rayon.

Keenson and Company
Room 1706, Wing Tuck Commercial Centre
177-183 Wing Lok Street, West
Hong Kong
All kinds shopping, travelling, cosmetic &
toilet bags made of various materials.

Kingdar Enterprises Limited
Flat 6, 14/F., Wah Fat Industrial Building
10-14 Kung Yip Street
Kwai Chung, Hong Kong
All kinds travelling bags, sports bags,
cosmetic bags, handbags, purses, made of
cotton, nylon, PU, PVC, velvet, etc.

Kingsway Mfg. Co.
Flat B, 8/F., Tin Wui Industrial Building
No. 3, Hing Wong Road, Sun On Street
Tuen Mun, N.T., Hong Kong
Gold electroplating evening handbags with
rhinestones for decoration & acrylic, lucite
evening handbags.

Kwan Yick Corporation
Waylee Industrial Centre
B7, D7 & D13, Tsuen King Circuit
Tsuen Wan, N.T., Hong Kong
Polyethylene braided & woven shopping
bags, polyethylene & polypropylene mesh
bags & woven bags for packing potatoes,
onions, chemicals & fertilizers, with or
without printing.

Lily Royce Manufacturing Co. Ltd.
901 Humphrey's Building,
9/F., 11 Humphrey's Avenue, Tsimshatsui
Kowloon, Hong Kong
Metal evening handbags with semi-precious
stones for decoration, metal with snake-skin
& silk brocade evening handbags.

Leif Lowe Manufacturing Ltd.
G/F., Ka Chau Industrial Building
6 Sheung Hei Street, Sanpokong
Kowloon, Hong Kong
Ladies' metal handbags, gold/silver plated.

Lloyd Pascoe Leather Craft (H.K.) Co. Ltd.
2/F., Luen Tai Industrial Building
72-76 Kwai Cheong Road
Kwai Chung, N.T., Hong Kong
Wide range of leather goods, leading
leatherware manufacturer with 27 years
experience.

Splendour Industrial Company
Flat B, 4/F., Hing Win Fty. Building
110 How Ming Street
Kwun Tong
Kowloon, Hong Kong
Water items, medicated water in assorted
colours & anti-frozen, water beach bags,
school bags, cosmetic bags & sun-visors, etc.

Sunny Handbag Industrial Co. Toniway Co.
Room 3502 Singga Commercial Centre
148 Connaught Road, West
Hong Kong
Canvas bags, PVC bags, pencil cases, etc.

Sun Lick Manufactory
20-24 Bute Street, 6/F.
Fook Chiu Factory Building
Kowloon, Hong Kong
All kinds purses & wallets made of PU &
PVC.

Tai Hing International (Trading) Ltd.
308-9 International Building
141 Des Voeux Road, Central
Hong Kong
Ladies' evening handbags & belts made of
glass beads.

Tung Sun Industrial Company
127/135 Yeung Uk Road, 4/F.
Tsuen Wan, N.T., Hong Kong
All kinds bags, including 5 piece oxford
nylon travelling set.

V & E Enterprises Limited
8/F., "A" Minden House
13-15 Minden Avenue, Tsimshatsui
Kowloon, Hong Kong
Small leather goods.

Universal Trading Co.
Room 2004, Blk. N, Telford Garden
Kowloon Bay
Kowloon, Hong Kong
Light-weight colorful wallets (in oxford
nylon), coin-purses & key holders.

lWai Chung Beading Co.
27 Kok Cheung Street, Blk. C, 12/F.
Tai Kok Tsui
Kowloon, Hong Kong
Handmade ladies' beaded evening handbags
& purses, ladies' silk beaded/sequined
evening dress, full range of petit-point
handbags, rayon satin & rayon brocade
evening bags & hand embroidered pictures.

Wiebo & Co.
13 Li Yuen Street, West, 10/F., Central
Cosmetic bags, shopping bags, fashion bags,
purses, pencil cases, wallets.

Wing Kwong Polyethylene & Printing Fty.
Lung Shing Industrial Building, 7/F., Flat B
142-148 Texaco Road
Tsuen Wan, N.T., Hong Kong
High & low density polyethylene products
ranging from Christmas & household table
cloths to vest bags, shopping carrier bags,
food bags, butcher bags with lids, deep
freeze bags, garbage bags, waste bin liners,
garment covers, bags & tubing, Christmas
gift bags.

Wincos Enterprise
1005 Leader Commercial Building
54 Hillwood Road, Tsimshatsui
Kowloon, Hong Kong
Ladies' evening bags.

Ying Ho Industrial Co. Ltd.
15/F., Blk. B, Mai Shun Industrial Building
18-24 Kwai Cheong Road
Kwai Chung, N.T., Hong Kong
Plastic mirrors, lighted make-up mirrors,
cosmetic mirror/brush sets & all other
mirrors & handbags.

Ying Kit Handbag Manufactory
Flat C, 1/F., Hong Kong Industrial Building
444-452 Des Voeux Road, West
Hong Kong
Ladies' fashion handbags, purses, cosmetic
bags & disco bags, made of jacquard,
velveteen, PU.

Hung Fung Co. Ltd.
9 Walnut Street, Taikoktsui
Kowloon, Hong Kong
Steel/brass pressure lanterns divided into
rapid type & alcohol type, kerosene stoves &
brass pressure stoves.

An Tat Tools Works Ltd.
Kingsway Industrial Building
9/F., Blk. G & H, 10/F., Blk. E
173 Wo Yi Hop Road
Kwai Chung, N.T., Hong Kong
Screwdriver sets & tools.

Calenway Company
Room 105, Wing Fu Building
22-24 Wing Kut Street
Kong Kong
Builder's hardware & door fittings.

Chung Fai Metal & Plastic Fty.
City Industrial Complex, 13/F., Flat C
116-122 Kwok Shui Road
Kwai Chung, N.T., Hong Kong
Screwdriver sets & tools for over 18 years.
Chrome vanadium & carbon steel.

Hang Shun Metal & Plastic Manufactory
Flat A & C, 3/F., Wah Fung Industrial
Centre
Blk. 1, 33-39 Kwai Fung Street
Kwai Chung, N.t., Hong Kong
Screwdriver sets & tools, made of steel,
nickel & copper.

Hung Lee International Ltd.
Man On Building, 11/F., Blk. A
Hong Kong
Key chains.

Kit Loong & Co.
G.P.O. Box 7951
Hong Kong
Switchblade items, clip knives, nail files with
iron keychain, ball pen & moustache comb
with iron keychain, flick combs & other
switchblade items.

Kwan Ngai Metal Fty.
11/F., Flat B2, Phase 1
Tsing Yi Industrial Centre, Lot No. 65
Tsing Yi Island, Hong Kong
Pocket knives, letter openers & scissors.

Wei Cheong Metalware Factory Ltd.
5/F., Yip Fung Industrial Building, Blk.
A2-4
28-36 Kwai Fung Crescent
Kwai Chung, N.T., Hong Kong
Parts for all kinds of ornaments.

Wing Tat Wall Picture Mfy.
211 Tong Hing Road, Tai Tau Ling
Sheung Shui, N.t., Hong Kong
Christmas decorations, candles/oil lamps,
decorative stainless steel bar sets.

Foretrade International Co.
Central P.O. Box 70740
Kowloon,, Hong Kong
Polyethylene gloves, aprons, showercaps,
raincoats, shopping bags, garbage bags,
PVC shoecovers, mattress covers.

Hop Shing Plastics Manufacture Fty.
8 Tung Shing Lane
Yuen Long, N.T., Hong Kong
Hospital disposable products, P.E. gloves,
arm gloves aprons, caps & bath hoods.

Luen Wor Cosmetic Fty. Ltd.
Block G, 12/F., City Industrial Complex
116-122 Kwok Shui Road
Kwai Chung, N.T., Hong Kong
Medicated oil & essential balm.

New World Industrial Fty.
Flat D, 12/F., 41-43 Au Pui Wan Street
On Wah Industrial Building
Fo Tan Village
Shatin, N.T., Hong Kong
Electric body & foot massager, massage
sandals, slimmer belts, breast developers,
massage pillows, facial massagers & magnetic
bracelets/necklaces.

Bonnet & Cape Manufactory Ltd.
Flat A, 4/F., Blk. 1, Camelpaint Building
62 Hoi Yuen Road, Kwun Tong
Kowloon, Hong Kong
Folded type nylon food covers, PVC & PE
bowl & pot covers made to buyers' own
sizes.

Domestic Chemical Products Ltd.
19/F., Jing Ho Industrial Building
78-84 Wang Lung Street
Tsuen Wan, N.T., Hong Kong
Household cleansing products, deodorants,
naphthalene moth balls, detergent powder,
liquid detergent, power cleanser, shampoo.

Effect Trading Co.
room 402, Yue's House
306 Des Voeux Road, Central
Hong Kong
Metal/plastic/nylon kithen-ware, hand-tools.

F.C.C. & Company
P.O. Box 95783, Tsimshatsui Post Office
Kowloon, Hong Kong
"F.C.C." brand of vinyl lace, plastic
doilies, placemats & table cloths.

Kwong Tai Lamp Fty. Ltd.
Blk. A, 1/F., Kingsway Industries Building
167-171 Wo Yi Hop Road
Kwai Chung, N.T., Hong Kong
Lamp burners, kerosene lamps & candle
lamps with candles.

Lap Fai Machinery & Metal Fty.
Blk. 1, Flat B, 6/F.
Yee Lim Industrial Building
32-40 Kwai Ting Road
Kwai Chung, N.t., Hong Kong
Automatic button attaching machine,
automatic riveting machine & eyelet
punching machine, also snap buttons, rivets,
trouser hooks, eyelets, battery caps, buckles,
etc.

Luen Cheong Can Factory Limited
60 Hung To Road, G/F., Kwun Tong
Kowloon, Hong Kong
Cans to fit almost every customer's
requirements for chocolate, biscuit, tea, oil
& petroleum cans. Decorative service trays,
canister sets & screw caps.

Man Yee Can Co. (HK) Ltd.
4 Dai Fu Street, Tai Po Industrial Estate
Tai Po, N.T., Hong Kong
Tinplate lithographer/manufacturer
decorative service trays, canister sets,
advertising posters, screw caps & tinplate
containers for packing chocolate, biscuits,
milk powder, curry powder, brilliantine &
lubricating oil.

Mayfair Company
Room 1801, 18/F.
Lee Wai Commercial Building
1-3A Hart Avenue, Tsimshatsui
Kowloon, Hong Kong
Hand tools, e.g., plastic dust collector, drain
pipe cleaner & plastic multi-function pliers.

Sachen Electric Bulb Fty. Ltd.
12/F., Flat C1, Hang Fung Industrial
Building
2G Hok Yuen Street, Hunghom
Kowloon, Hong Kong
Neon testing screwdrivers, mains testers,
voltage testers, circuit continuity testers.
Also deal with miniature bulbs & Christmas
light sets.

T. Wilson Trading Limited
Room 403, Landwide Commercial Building
118-120 Austin Road
Kowloon, Hong Kong
Handtools & auto accessories.

Tung Tack Lee
55 Wellington Street
Hong Kong
Wooden rulers & builders' hardware.

Hong Fuk Co.
Blk. E, 12/F., Sui Sham Industrial Building
8-10 Kwai Shau Road
Kwai Chung, N.T., Hong Kong
All kinds of mobiles, hanging, tale, ball tree
car & plastic miniatures in different models.

Islandcan LImited
13/F., Granville House, 41C
Granville Road, Tsimshatsui
Kowloon, Hong Kong
Decorative tinware. Canister sets, trays &
coasters, promotional items.

Inter-Pacific Supplies Co. Ltd.
G.P.O. Box No. 2664
Hong Kong
Collection of tinsel garlands & Christmas
decorations.

Johnny Supplies Ltd.
Flat A3, 14/F., Hankow Centre
47, Peking Road, Tsimshatsui
Kowloon, Hong Kong
Artificial green foliages, flowering plants,
flower bouquets & bushes, feathered birds &
items, cake decorations, party favours &
year round festival novelties.

King's Industrial Corp.
1601, Wanchai Commercial Centre
194-204 Johnston Road
Hong Kong
Travel kits, toilet kits for men, women,
amenities for hotels, guest-rooms & airlines
passengers, also slippers, eye-shades, shower
caps.

Kimberway Limited
Flat B, 5/F., Prat Commercial Building
17-19 Prat Avenue, Tsimshatsui
Kowloon, Hong Kong
Fine silver, gold, chrome-plated giftware,
especially trays, candlesticks & other
tableware.

Kit Hart Metal Factory
Kwai Tak Industrial Building
Blk. 1, 4/F., Flat C & D
Kwai Tak Road
Kwai Chung, N.T., Hong Kong
All kinds of gold & silver-plated metal &
brass buckles & buttons for belts & bags.

Lamco Merchandising Company
Room 810, Li Po Chun Chambers
185-195 Des Voeux Road, C.
Hong Kong
Toys, gifts & decorative articles.

Leif Lowe Manufacturing Ltd.
G/F., Ka Chau Industrial Building
6 Sheung Hei Street, Sanpokong
Kowloon, Hong Kong
All kinds ladies' metal handbags, gold/silver
plated.

Dickie Plastic Fty. Ltd.
Flat C, 11/F., Shui Wing Industrial Building
12-22 Tai Yuen Street
Kwai Chung, N.T., Hong Kong
Candy novelties & candy containers for all
seasons.

Yuk Sung Industrial Corporation
9/F., Lyton Building
46 Mody Road, Tsimshatsui
Kowloon, Hong Kong
Auto-lit cigarette case combined with
cigarette case lighter & ash-tray in plastic
cabinet.

Everwin Industrial Mfy.
Blk. D, 22/F.
Melbourne Industrial Building
16 Westland Road
Quarry Bay, Hong Kong
Metal & plastic giftware, souvenirs,
advertising premiums.

Floral Trends Ltd.
Unit 501 Houston Centre, 63 Mody Road
Tsimshatsui East
Kowloon, Hong Kong
Florals, foliage & Christmas decor.

Genuine Associates (Sundries) Ltd.
51 Man Yue Street, Kaiser Estate (Phase 2)
Top Floor, Flat L
Kowloon, Hong Kong
All kinds of home decorations & wooden
housewares, wooden/metal framed pictures
& pub-mirrors, glass decorative plaques,
plastic/aluminum photo frames.

Hong Kong Candles Manufactory
Blk. 19, 16/F.
Wah Luen Industrial Building
15-21 Wong Chuk Yeung Street
Fo Tan
Shatin, N.T., Hong Kong
Birthday, relight, party candles.

Highlands Silver Plate Co. Ltd.
Room 913, Nan Fung Centre
TWTL 258, Castle Peak Road
Tsuen Wan, N.T., Hong Kong
Silverplated, goldplated & brassplate
giftware & tableware, custom made projects
such as trophies, pitchers & commemorative
plate in the silverplate & goldplate,
inscriptions of name, logo & scenes can be
done on most items.

Hoda Company
G.P.O. Box 10153
Hong Kong
Oil & traditional Chinese paintings with a
variety of subjects. Portraits from individual
photos & copies of old masters.

Luen Bond Manufactory Company
Room 308, Kar Wong Building
639-645 Shanghai Street
Kowloon, Hong Kong
Electronic musical products, melody cards, toys, watches, door bells, musical boxes, paper organs, musical bells, fun faces with music & calculators.

Maxim Novelty Co. Ltd.
Room 704, Hanford House
221D & E, Nathan Road
Kowloon, Hong Kong
Polyester & plastic artificial flowers, plants, bushes, foliage, Christmas decorations, arrangements & baskets.

Ma's Flower Design
588-592, Castle Peak Road
Winsum Industrial Building, No. 7, 2/F.
Kowloon, Hong Kong
Hand made artificial silk flowers, novelties & arrangements.

May Cheong Plastiic Manufactory Ltd.
7 Ngau Tau Kok Road, 4/F.
Amoycan Industrial Building
Kowloon, Hong Kong
Mirrors, plastic vacuum plating, florentine & classy designs of purse framed mirror-combs.

Ming Shing Plastic & Metal Fty. Ltd.
42, Lee Chung Street, G/F.
Cheung Wei Industrial Building
Chaiwan, Hong Kong
Acrylic key chains, bottle opener with magnetic back, key chain with ball pens.

Ming Shing Plastic & Metal Fty. Ltd.
42, Lee Chung Street, G/F.
Cheung Wei Industrial Building
Chaiwan, Hong Kong
Acrylic key chains & other items.

Modern Art Products Co.
Harvard House, 9/F., 106-111 Thomson Road
Wanchai, Hong Kong
Chinese water-colour artwork on cork-paper, high quality original oil paintings of landscapes, seascapes, florals, street scenes, harbour scenes, still-life & portraits.

New Kid Metal Die Casting Manufactory Ltd.
4/F., B 11, Blk. B
Hong Kong Industrial Centre
489-491 Castle Peak Road, Lai Chi Kok
Kowloon, Hong Kong
Toys & gold-plated keychains, ideal for premiums, gifts & advertising purposes.

Multi Trading Company
Room 301 & 305, Kimberley House
35 Kimberley Road
Kowloon, Hong Kong
New production "Hand spray oil paintings on canvas, framed & unframed."

Pata Industry Company
Aluminum photo frames, surface finish in gold, solver & bronze, also diagonal line with black, maroon & grey.

Pleasant Metal Works Limited
Flat A, 3/F., Blk. 4
Gold Dragon Industrial Centre
Tai Lin Pai Road
Kwai Chung, N.T., Hong Kong
Metal & plastic key holders, bottle openers, pins & badges. Specialized in advertising, specialties, giveaways.

Poss Trading Centre Ltd.
7/F., Parder House
72 Queen's Road, Central
Hong Kong
Bridal accessories, including hair decorations, gloves, lacy containers, fans, flower bouquets.

Samson Industrial Corp.
G.P.O. Box 11071
Hong Kong
Novelty tape-measures, key-chains & magnifiers

Siu Hing Cheung Metal Manufactory Limited
Blk. C, G/F., Wah Fung Industrial Centre
33-39 Kwai Fung Crescent
Kwai Chung, N.T., Hong Kong
Metal, brass & die casting products.

Tai Tung Co.
Unit 9, 3/F., Kinglet Industrial Building
21-23 Shing Wan Road
Tai Wai, Shatin, N.T., Hong Kong
All kinds of plastic jewelery boxes.

Tinilite Industries
3 Kin Kwan Street
Winfield Industrial Building, 4/F., Blk. H
Tuen Mun, N.T., Hong Kong
Flashlights with keychains.

The Toytrade Distribution Ltd.
1001-2 Far East Consortium Building
121 Des Voeux Road, Central
Hong Kong
Travel with care set, made for Croner Toy in Australia under licence.

Tysun & Chow Company
109-112 Gloucester Road
Tung Wai Commercial Building, 8/F.
Wanchai, Hong Kong
Christmas decoration novelties from small tree ornaments to large display articles, beaded chains, mirror ornaments, feather birds, Valentine, Easter & Mother's Day items.

Chapter Fifteen

Publications For Your Advertising Campaign

FAMILY WEEKLY
641 Lexington Ave.
New York, NY 10022

AMERICAN BUSINESS
1775 Broadway
New York, NY 10019

MONEY
Rockefeller Center
New York, NY 10020

POPULAR SCIENCE
380 Lexington Ave.
New York, NY 10017

SUCCESS UNLIMITED
401 N. Wabash Ave.
Chicago, IL 60611

VENTURE
35 W. 45th St.
New York, NY 10036

ENTREPRENEUR
2311 Ponitus Ave.
Los Angeles, CA 90064

WALL STREET JOURNAL
22 Cortlandt
New York, NY 10007

WORKBENCH
4251 Pennsylvania Ave.
Kansas City, MO 64111

FIREHOUSE
515 Madison Ave.
New York, NY 10022

PARADE
750 Third Ave.
New York, NY 10017

TIME
1271 Avenue of the Americas
New York, NY 10020

MOTHER EARTH NEWS
105 Stoney Mt. Rd.
Hendersonville, NC 28739

NEW YORK TIMES
229 W. 43rd St.
New York, NY 10036

SIGNATURE
880 Third Ave.
New York, NY 10022

AMERICAN WAY
488 Madison Ave.
New York, NY 10022

TWA AMBASSADOR
1999 Shepard Rd.
St. Paul, MN 55116

UNITED MAINLINER
5900 Wilshire Blvd.
Los Angeles, CA 90036

AMERICAN LEGION MAGAZINE
700 N. Penn St.
Indianapolis, IN 46206

COLUMBIA
78 Meadow St.
New Haven, CT 06510

EAGLE MAGAZINE
425 W. Diversey Pkwy.
Chicago, IL 60614

KIWANIS
101 E. Erie St.
Chicago, IL 60611

FUTURE
P.O. Box 7
Tulsa, OK 74121

MOOSE MAGAZINE
100 E. Ohio St.
Chicago, IL 60611

SERGEANTS
4235 28th Ave.
Marlow Heights, MD 20031

VFW MAGAZINE
406 W. 34th St.
Kansas City, MO 64111

STAR
730 Third Ave.
New York, NY 10017

TWO EXCELLENT DIRECTORIES FOR IMPORTED ITEMS

MADE IN EUROPE
P.O. Box 170402
D-6000 Frankfurt/M. 1
West Germany

HONG KONG ENTERPRISE
333 N. Michigan Ave.
Chicago, IL 60601